JAN

D0599605

Cuba

Cuba

BY DAVID K. WRIGHT

Enchantment of the World™
Second Series

Children's Press®

An Imprint of Scholastic Inc.

NEW YORK   TORONTO   LONDON   AUCKLAND   SYDNEY
MEXICO CITY   NEW DELHI   HONG KONG
DANBURY, CONNECTICUT

Frontispiece: El Morro fortress at the mouth of Havana Bay

Consultant: Richard Abisla, International Observer, Civic Council of Grassroots and
Indigenous Groups of Honduras

Please note: All statistics are as up-to-date as possible at the time of publication.

Book production by Herman Adler

Library of Congress Cataloging-in-Publication Data

Wright, David K.
 Cuba / by David K. Wright.
    p. cm.—(Enchantment of the world. Second series)
 Includes bibliographical references and index.
 ISBN-13: 978-0-531-12096-5
 ISBN-10: 0-531-12096-1
 1. Cuba—Juvenile literature. I. Title. II. Series.
 F1785.W75 2008
 972.91—dc22   2008008423

Cuba

Contents

Cover photo:
A Cuban schoolgirl

Escambray Mountains

Cuban children

Welcome to Cuba

Fidel Castro speaks in
Havana in 1981.

Opposite: **A field of tobacco
grows in the Valle de Viñales
in eastern Cuba.**

MOST PEOPLE HAVE HEARD OF FIDEL CASTRO. HE was the leader of Caribbean island nation of Cuba for almost half a century, from 1959 until his retirement in 2008. Yet, in Cuba, a nineteenth-century writer and journalist, José Martí, is just as famous as Castro. It was Martí who provided Castro with many of his ideas.

In Martí's time, Cuba was a Spanish colony. Many Cubans resented the fact that Spain had been treating Cuba harshly for hundreds of years. Martí was not the first to propose that Cuba revolt and become independent, but he may have made the case for independence better and more convincingly than anyone else. Thus, many Cubans think of Martí as the father of their country.

From his boyhood, Martí opposed the heavy-handed Spanish government and injustices such as slavery. While plotting Cuba's independence, he traveled to Europe, the United States, and Central America. He also became a lawyer and studied philosophy and painting.

Martí returned to Cuba with a number of soldiers. He was determined to overthrow the Spaniards, but he was killed in his first battle. Today, outside Cuba, he is perhaps best known for writing some of the poetic words in the popular song "Guantanamera." That tune reminds many people of Martí's beautiful island.

The Escambray Mountains rise in south-central Cuba.

Cuba is the largest island in the Caribbean Sea. It lies between the Gulf of Mexico and the Atlantic Ocean, a mere 90 miles (145 kilometers) from the southern tip of Florida.

Cuba is long and thin. It measures 708 miles (1,139 km) east to west but is only 135 miles (217 km) north to south. Both ends of the island are mountainous, while much of the rest of Cuba is fertile, low-lying farmland. Cuba is lined with beautiful beaches and quiet coves and attracts many international visitors.

A woman enjoys the white sand beaches on Cayo Largo, an island south of mainland Cuba.

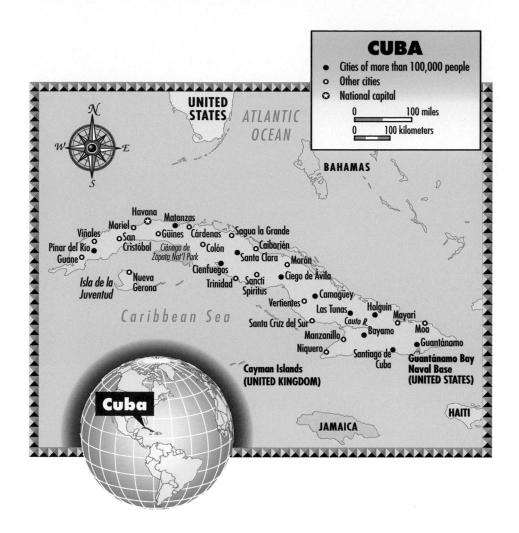

A Communist Nation

Cuba gets few visitors from the United States, which bans most of its citizens from traveling there. That's partly because of the kind of government Cuba has. Cuba is one of the few communist nations in the world. Under communism, a nation has a strong central government that controls the economy and owns almost all businesses. For forty-nine years, Cuba was governed by one man, President Fidel Castro. Some people believe that Castro found the best possible way to

Fulgencio Batista seized control of Cuba in 1952 and ruled the country as a dictator. He fled Cuba at the end of 1958, when it became apparent that the revolution was going to be successful.

govern Cuba. Others believe that the Cuban people will not be truly free so long as their nation has a communist government.

Castro brought communism to the island in 1959, after he led a successful revolution. The country was ready for change—it had been run by a dictator named Fulgencio Batista, and corruption was widespread. Today, Cuba has less corruption, but it also has less food, a housing shortage, and little money.

A Tourist Destination

Visitors to modern Cuba find things to like and to dislike. Most appreciate the music, the safe streets, the absence of racism, and the high level of education. But they also notice the crumbling buildings, the drab apartment complexes, and the shortages of many basic goods.

Cubans have always thought of themselves as independent—even when ruled by foreigners. They are also aware that their island is beautiful and that tourists from many places in the world find Cuba special. The Cuban people are well read, and they excel at several sports, music, and other arts.

Uncertain Future

More than eleven million people live in Cuba. There are also hundreds of thousands of Cuban Americans living in Florida and elsewhere. They fled the island because they disagreed with Castro's 1959 revolution.

By 2006, Castro was too ill to continue with his duties as president of Cuba. He officially resigned in 2008, and his brother Raúl, who was seventy-six years old at the time, took over. Will Raúl Castro continue to run the country as Fidel did? Or will the change in leadership signal a newer Cuba with more freedoms and adequate food, housing, and money? The world waits and watches.

Raúl Castro officially succeeded his brother as president on February 24, 2008.

A Grand Island

MANY SMALL CARIBBEAN ISLANDS ARE FLAT CHUNKS of sand and coral. Cuba, in contrast, offers varied terrain. No matter where they live, Cubans usually have sweeping views. Many say they miss the landscape whenever they leave.

Cuba is the largest island in the Caribbean. The country is 42,804 square miles (110,861 sq km), about the size of the state of Pennsylvania and a little smaller than the nation of Greece.

Opposite: **The Valle de los Ingenios, near the city of Trinidad, was a center of sugarcane cultivation in the 1700s and 1800s.**

Palms form an arch over a beach in Varadero. The town is a popular vacation destination for travelers from around the world.

Cuba stretches about 700 miles (1,100 km) across the Caribbean. It is physically similar to the Caribbean's other large islands, such as Hispaniola (an island shared by the Dominican Republic and Haiti) and Puerto Rico. Together, these islands are known as the Greater Antilles. Smaller islands to the east and south are known as the Lesser Antilles. Thousands of tiny islands along Cuba's coast belong to Cuba, as does a large island, Isla de la Juventud, off the southwest coast.

Cuba's Geographic Features

Area: 42,804 square miles (110,861 sq km)

Greatest Distance East to West: 708 miles (1,139 km)

Greatest Distance North to South: 135 miles (217 km)

Bordering Countries: None

Highest Elevation: Pico Turquino, 6,542 feet (1,994 m)

Lowest Elevation: Sea level, along the coast

Longest River: Cauto River, 155 miles (249 km)

Average High Temperatures: In Havana, 89°F (32°C) in August; 75°F (24°C) in January

Average Annual Rainfall: More than 70 inches (180 cm) in the mountains, 40 inches (100 cm) in the lowlands

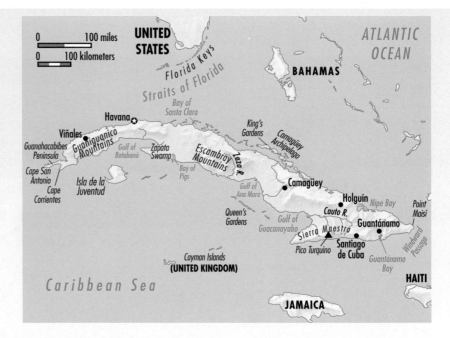

Havana sits on Cuba's northern coast, along the Gulf of Mexico.

The Lowlands

About three-quarters of Cuba consists of rolling plains. This rich land is good for farming. The island has many bays that reach inland, making it easy to transport farm products by boat. Most of Cuba's major cities grew up along the coast.

The capital city of Havana lies on a bay on the northern coast. It has been an important port since it was founded by the Spanish in the early 1500s. East of the capital are broad, flat, fertile fields that prove ideal for growing sugarcane. The Bay of Santa Clara is home to top tourist attractions: beaches, hotels, and dozens of cays, or tiny islands or reefs, where tourists find the scuba diving ideal. The country's busiest highway links the cities here to Havana.

The Valle de Viñales features many limestone hills.

One of the lushest parts of Cuba is the Valle de Viñales (Valley of Vines), a tobacco-growing center on the far west end of the island. The valley includes soaring rock formations, limestone caves, and a farm village, Viñales, that seems to have changed little in hundreds of years. Low but dramatic limestone hills dot the valley.

Cuba's best beaches are strewn like a string of pearls around Isla de la Juventud, a large island off the southwestern coast. Ancient people made many line drawings, called petroglyphs, on the rocks there. Juventud is largely swampy but has many orchards of citrus fruit. Old shipwrecks fill the nearby waters.

The central southern coast features pristine wetlands, vast fields of crops, and miles of unspoiled beaches. Migratory waterfowl come here in the winter, settling among the many saltwater lagoons. Zapata Swamp, the largest swamp in Cuba, is in this area.

A Visit to Zapata Swamp

The largest wetlands area in the Caribbean is Zapata Swamp in Cuba's Matanzas Province. Part of the swamp is protected as Ciénaga de Zapata National Park. The swamp has been compared to Florida's Everglades. The huge, wet, low-lying area is a rich mix of swamps and grasslands. The secluded area is the perfect place for birds, reptiles, and mammals to bear their young.

Zapata Swamp is home to about 900 plant species, about 900 fish species, 172 bird species, 31 different kinds of reptiles, and more than 1,000 kinds of invertebrate animals. It is one of only two places where the Cuban crocodile survives.

Zapata Swamp is also a top fishing spot, and many bird-watchers visit the wet wilderness. There, they can see everything from bee hummingbirds—the world's smallest bird—to majestic hawks and colorful parrots.

Coral reefs and empty beaches attract visitors farther east, in the provinces of Ciego de Ávila and Camagüey. These sparsely populated regions are mostly flat and were formerly forested. Residents of tiny villages take tourists fishing and sightseeing among a series of offshore islands called Queen's Gardens ("Jardines de la Reina" in Spanish). A matching King's Gardens ("Jardines del Rey") lies off the northern coast.

Parts of southeastern Cuba are dry and hot. This includes Guantánamo, a U.S. military base near the eastern end of the island. Cuba began leasing the Guantánamo base to the U.S. government in 1903. After Fidel Castro came to power, some Cubans wanted to take Guantánamo back, but nothing was done.

American soldiers march at Guantánamo. The U.S. naval base there covers 45 square miles (117 sq km).

Clouds cloak the Sierra Maestra in southeastern Cuba.

The Mountains

The sawtoothed Sierra Maestra are the outstanding feature of eastern Cuba. The mountain range's tallest peak, Pico Turquino, rises 6,542 feet (1,994 meters) along the southeastern coast. The country's longest river, the Cauto, starts in the Sierra Maestra and flows for 155 miles (249 km) before emptying into the Gulf of Guacanayabo on the southern coast.

Farther west, the Escambray Mountains loom over the city of Trinidad. They are shorter than the Sierra Maestra, reaching about 3,380 feet (1,150 m) above sea level, and they boast many gushing waterfalls. In the far west are the Guaniguanico Mountains. Shorter still, their peaks rise to heights of about 2,500 feet (800 m).

People travel by boat following a severe flood in the city of Isabel Rubio in 2006.

Climate

Cuba is warm year-round. In Havana, the average high temperature in August is 89 degrees Fahrenheit (32 degrees Celsius), while in January, the average high is 75°F (24°C). Humidity makes the air feel even hotter in the summer, but winds off the ocean provide some relief.

Cuba receives an average of 52 inches (132 centimeters) of rain a year. Most of that rain falls during the rainy season, from May until October. Different parts of the country receive vastly different amounts of rain. The northeastern coast gets more rain than anywhere else on the island. Plants grow wildly in this area. After passing the northeastern coast, winds carrying clouds run into the soaring Sierra Maestra. By the time the air crosses over the mountains, all the rain has

Horrible Hurricanes

Many destructive hurricanes hit Cuba in the last century. Here are a few of the worst:

- November 9, 1932. Winds of almost 150 miles per hour (250 kph) hit the island, resulting in 3,033 deaths and waves on the southern coast as high as 20 feet (6 m).
- October 8, 1944. With winds clocked at 163 miles per hour (262 kph) and heavy rain, this storm killed about 300 people.
- October 4–7, 1963. Hurricane Flora flooded the eastern Sierra Maestra, killing about 1,000 people and ruining vast areas of crops. Flora forced Castro's new government to develop a modern weather service to better predict and warn people of coming storms.
- March 13, 1993. This was a rare spring storm. It wiped out entire plantations, devastating the sugar harvest, and damaged thirty thousand homes.

fallen from it and the clouds have disappeared. The southern side of the range is so dry that cactuses are common. Cuba's second-largest city, Santiago de Cuba, lies in this dry region on the southern coast.

During the late summer and fall, Cubans search the skies for hurricanes, powerful tropical storms that form along the coast of Africa and move west across the Atlantic Ocean. Packing high winds and heavy rain, these storms, if they hit land, can be extremely destructive and deadly. They erode beaches, destroy houses and fields, and wash out roads. Cuba receives a direct blow from a hurricane about once every two years.

This satellite image shows Tropical Storm Ernesto hovering over Cuba in August 2006.

Saving the Environment

Cuba is filled with lovely landscapes. People travel from all over the world to enjoy its beaches and mountains and admire its birds and sea life. But like many places around the world, Cuba suffers from serious pollution. Old cars belch exhaust through the streets of Havana. Air pollutants pour out of huge sugar refineries and cement factories. Sewage and industrial pollution that pours into the waters threatens sea life.

The Cuban government needs the country's economy to grow, but it also recognizes that protecting the environment is important, both for its own sake and to maintain the tourist industry. In 2002, Castro said, "Society's needs can be met without destroying nature and basic human values." The Cuban government is working to improve the environment. Havana Harbor and the Almendares River, which cuts through Havana, have both undergone a huge cleanup effort. The people of Havana have seen the waters clear up as a result.

Pollution pours from a nickel factory near Moa, which is near the eastern end of the island.

Looking at Cuba's Cities

Havana is Cuba's capital and largest city, with a population of 2,686,000. The nation's second-largest city, with 554,400 residents, is Santiago de Cuba (above), often called simply Santiago. It is on the southeastern part of the island in a dry region that sometimes goes for months without rain. Santiago boasts wide boulevards, handsome plazas, historic buildings, vibrant people, and ever-present music.

Camagüey (left), which has a population of 354,400, is one of the island's oldest settlements. It lies about midway between Havana and Santiago. The city boasts a mazelike layout that was intended to confuse the pirates who frequently attacked the city in the 1500s. Visitors wandering its narrow streets will discover many lovely churches and grand buildings.

Cuba's fourth-largest city is Holguín, with a population of 319,300. Holguín is set amid rolling hills north of Santiago. It has a handsome center city that dates to colonial times and is surrounded by newer buildings.

A Grand Island **27**

Extraordinary Life

THE WATERS AROUND CUBA HAVE NOT BEEN OVERFISHED. Consequently, the widest variety of sea life in the Western Hemisphere lives in the warm waters near the island. Schools of brightly colored fish dart around snorkelers and scuba divers. Eels, rays, jellyfish, barracudas, bonefish, and hundreds of other species also live in the area. In all, Cuba's waters are home to more than five hundred saltwater species.

Opposite: **The leopard dwarf boa is native to Cuba. It kills prey by squeezing it to death.**

The coral reefs near Cuba are home to amazing sea life, such as this cluster of feather duster worms.

What makes the waters around the large island so inviting? Part of the answer is coral. Coral polyps are tiny, reef-building creatures. Their skeletons make up the hard reef. Living coral, meanwhile, is delicate and colorful. Coral reefs provide many good hiding places for fish and other sea creatures, keeping smaller creatures safe from large predator fish.

Coral thrives in warm, shallow water. It is extremely sensitive to changes in the temperature and composition of the water. Even slight changes in the water can kill coral. Pollution has ruined coral around the world, but much of the coral around Cuba is healthy.

In deeper water near Cuba, large fish such as sharks, dolphins, tunas, marlins, and swordfish can be seen. The waters around Cuba are also home to sea turtles. On some summer nights, the turtles come ashore on Guanahacabibes Peninsula in the southwest to lay their eggs.

A healthy coral reef provides a habitat for many species, including gold striped goatfish.

Cuban hutias can weigh up to 19 pounds (8.5 kg).

Mammals and Other Creatures

Cuba is home to several unusual species. The hutia is a cat-sized rodent related to the guinea pig. These shy creatures forage for food at night. Another unusual animal is the solenodon. It grows about 12 inches (30 cm) long and has a pointed snout, which it uses to feed on insects and worms. Deer and wild boar also live in Cuba. Bats, which eat insects, can be found in Cuba's many caves and in buildings across the country.

Some Cuban mammals are considered pests. In the countryside, rats and mice eat grain that has been harvested. In the cities, they scour houses, streets, and parks looking for food.

The Trouble with Frogs

Some of Cuba's wildlife can be downright annoying. A constant source of trouble are tree frogs, which are found all over the island. If these small frogs get inside a house in their pursuit of insects to eat, they can do a great deal of damage. Tree frogs sometimes clog plumbing and damage electrical wiring.

Some animals in Cuba are in danger of extinction. One such mammal is the manatee, or sea cow. The first Europeans to reach the island mistook these large, harmless sea creatures for mermaids. Today, the manatee is endangered because it swims near the surface of the water and often becomes tangled in fishing nets or is hit by boat propellers.

Adult manatees weigh as much as 1,300 pounds (600 kg). They eat about 100 pounds (45 kg) of plant matter each day.

More than one hundred species of reptiles live in Cuba. Perhaps the most common reptile in Cuba is the tiny gecko, which people often see climbing walls inside houses. The nation's largest reptiles are alligators and crocodiles.

Cuba has no poisonous snakes. To many people, the nation's most intimidating snake is the Cuban boa, which can reach a length of 13 feet (4 m). It captures small mammals, squeezing and suffocating them before eating them.

Cuban crocodiles are found in only two places in the world: Zapata Swamp on mainland Cuba and Lanier Swamp on Isla de la Juventud.

Some of Cuba's most colorful wildlife is hard to spot. The island is known for the variety of snails, some with bright orange stripes, others yellow or glistening white. Each small shell is a little different than the next. Many Cuban children collect snail shells.

In the Air

In the cities of Cuba, one of the most common birds is the pigeon. Some are wild, and some are not. Some residents of Havana keep flocks of homing pigeons. They train them to fly away and then return home again.

Cuba also has many colorful birds. Flamingos, which have vivid pink feathers and long, thin bodies and legs, live all

The shells of Cuban tree snails often have bright stripes.

Cuban parrots sit atop a tree on the Guanahacabibes Peninsula in far western Cuba.

along the northern coast. They wade in the shallow water, searching for food. The flamingos get their pink hue from the tiny sea creatures they eat.

Other notable Cuban birds include the Cuban parrot, the Cuban trogon (the national bird), the Cuban parakeet, the Cuban cuckoo, the Zapata wren, and the Zapata rail. Many of these colorful species also live on other nearby Caribbean islands.

The Red, White, and Blue Bird

The national bird is the Cuban trogon, which Cubans call the *tocororo*. It is colored red, white, and blue, just like the Cuban flag. Trogons are about the size of a cardinal but have longer tail feathers.

Trogon is Greek for "nibbling." The birds' name comes from their habit of gnawing holes in trees to make their nests. Trogons do not migrate, and they seldom fly great distances. Instead, they use their broad bills to snatch fruit and insects as they fly from tree to tree. They sometimes dine on termites and then lay their eggs in the termites' former nest.

Extraordinary Life **35**

The Tallest Tree

The tall, stately royal palm is the national tree of Cuba. The royal palm was selected as the national tree because it grows throughout the country and is among the tallest trees on the island.

Royal palms range from 30 to 100 feet (10 to 30 m) tall. The trunks are white or nearly white, and they often have a bulge at their base or at the center of their trunk. Their leaves are sometimes more than 20 feet (6 m) long.

Royal palms cannot tolerate freezing weather, but they can withstand tropical storms. The trees easily shed their leaves in heavy winds, allowing them to stay upright in stormy weather.

Plant Life

At one time, forests covered almost all of Cuba. Over the centuries, people cut down many of the trees and replaced them with sugarcane and other crops. By 1950, only 14 percent of the land had forest. In recent years, Cuba has focused on preserving and renewing habitats. After much replanting, the island's proportion of forested land has now risen to almost 25 percent.

The tree most associated with Cuba is the stately royal palm, the national tree. Coconut palms and big belly palms also grow in great numbers.

Pine forests flourish on Isla de la Juventud and in the mountains of Cuba. Higher on the mountains are rain forests, where hardwood trees such as ebony and mahogany tower over ferns and other lush plants.

Butterfly Flowers

The national flower is the mariposa lily, which is tough and tender, versatile and beautiful. Related to the Easter lily and the tiger lily, the mariposa has three white petals around a gold-and-purple center. *Mariposa* means "butterfly" in Spanish, and it is the lily's markings that remind people of a butterfly. Mariposas give off a sweet fragrance.

Some stretches of the coast boast mangrove forests. Mangroves can grow in saltwater, which would kill most trees. The fingerlike roots of the mangrove rise out of the water and provide shelter for many small fish and birds.

Wildflowers abound across Cuba. They include spectacular orchids, bright bougainvilleas, and the richly scented mariposa lily, the national flower.

Mangroves growing in southern Cuba. Four different types of mangroves grow on the island.

CHAPTER

FOUR

Remote Times and Revolution

P EOPLE HAVE LIVED ON THE ISLAND OF CUBA FOR MORE than five thousand years. Cuba's earliest settlers are called the Ciboney people. Scientists believe that the Ciboney people migrated to Cuba from what is now Colombia, on the northern coast of South America. Their civilization left traces in Haiti, Puerto Rico, and Florida, and evidence suggests they were in Cuba as early as 3500 B.C. They hunted; gathered fruits, nuts, and other plant parts; and grew their own food. The Ciboney people were living in small villages all across the island when another group, the Taíno people, arrived.

Opposite: **Nearly 60 percent of Cuba's population is of mixed ethnicity.**

Cueva de Punta del Este

Isla de la Juventud is home to some of the most important Ciboney art in the Caribbean. Around A.D. 800, Ciboney people drew hundreds of pictures on the walls of a cave in the southeast of the island called Cueva de Punta del Este. The drawings are abstract and entirely red and black. They show circles within circles. Some experts believe that the paintings may be a kind of calendar.

Taínos Arrive

Scientists think that Taínos began arriving in Cuba around A.D. 900 and that they, too, migrated from South America. The Taínos eventually spread throughout the Caribbean. In Cuba, they pushed the Ciboney people off the fertile lowlands and into the mountains.

The Taíno people lived in villages and grew corn, potatoes, manioc (a starchy root also known as cassava), and tobacco. They also grew fruit such as guava, papaya, and pineapple. Fish were also a major part of the Taíno diet. Taínos sometimes traveled great distances in oceangoing canoes big enough to carry one hundred people.

Artifacts made by the Taíno people have been found on several Caribbean islands.

A Taíno village, complete with several huts, has been reconstructed at a site near Guardalavaca.

The Taíno people made sophisticated tools. They turned stones into knives and axes. They made clay pots and wove cloth. Taíno musical instruments included maracas, rattles, and hollow-log drums. Taínos housed all of these items in circular huts that were sometimes 20 feet (6 m) across.

By the 1400s, an estimated three hundred thousand Taínos and Ciboneys lived on Cuba. They would soon be joined by strangers from the east.

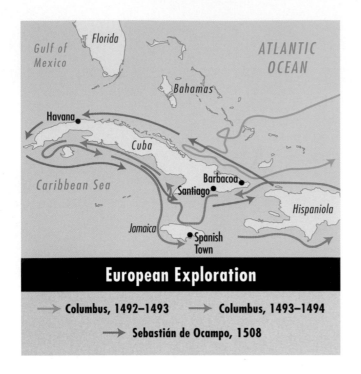

European Exploration

⟶ Columbus, 1492–1493   ⟶ Columbus, 1493–1494
⟶ Sebastián de Ocampo, 1508

Christopher Columbus, an Italian explorer working for Spain, set out from Europe in 1492 in search of a western route to Asia. He instead found Cuba. The island's lush landscape stunned Columbus. "The most beautiful land human eyes had ever seen," he called it. Columbus did not stay in Cuba long on his first visit, but he returned in 1494 and mapped part of Cuba's southern coast. Still, he did not realize that Cuba was an island. It wasn't until 1508, when a Spaniard named Sebastián de Ocampo sailed all the way around Cuba, that Europeans learned it was an island.

Christopher Columbus was the first European to explore Cuba.

Spain did not attempt to colonize Cuba until 1511. That year, Diego Velásquez de Cuéllar led three hundred Spanish soldiers in an invasion of mountainous eastern Cuba. The Spaniards wanted to conquer Cuba and gather riches for themselves and for the king of Spain.

The island's native people rallied around a Taíno named Hatuey. He had seen European cruelty on the nearby island of Hispaniola. Hatuey and others fought Velásquez valiantly, but they were no match for Spanish bullets and armor. Hatuey was captured and killed, signaling an end to the resistance.

The Spanish colonists treated the native people as virtual slaves, forcing them to work in mines and on plantations. The native population plummeted. Some people died from overwork, but many more died from European diseases such as measles and smallpox. Because these diseases had

Hatuey was burned at the stake in 1512 after being captured by conquistadores.

been common in Europe for centuries, many Europeans had built up immunity to them. Their bodies could fight the diseases. The Taínos and Ciboneys, however, had never been exposed to these diseases. When they came into contact with them, they became ill, and the diseases quickly spread. It is estimated that by 1550, only five thousand native Cubans remained.

Real Fuerza Castle was built in Havana in the late 1500s. It has thick walls and is surrounded by a moat.

Growth of a Colony

By 1522, the Taínos and Ciboneys were disappearing fast. That year, the Spanish brought the first enslaved Africans to Cuba to work on the plantations. The Spanish had captured the Africans and brought them to the Caribbean under terrible conditions in crowded ships.

By this time, Cuba was a vast farm. Coffee, sugarcane, and other crops grew quickly on the island. Much of the harvest left on ships bound for Spain. And Spain insisted that colonists on Cuba get all their goods from Spain. They could not trade with anyone else.

Havana, which was established on the site of what had once been a handsome Taíno village, became a major shipping port. Cuban sugar, cattle, tobacco, and timber went across the ocean to Spain. Ships heading for Spain from Mexico and Central and South America stopped in Havana. Many of them were carrying gold and other treasure.

All these riches began to attract pirates. They attacked Havana and other cities, stealing everything they could get their hands on. The pirates were a mix of nationalities, but many were English. Among the most notorious was Edward Teach (1680–1718), who was known as Blackbeard. A fierce fighter, he earned his nickname by lighting matches in and around his beard before a battle.

The Spanish built a ring of forts around the island to protect the ports, but they did little good. Meanwhile, the Spanish empire weakened. The English finally captured Havana's El Morro fortress in 1762. They then opened Havana to trade with other countries.

Eventually, more than a half million enslaved Africans were brought to Cuba. They harvested sugarcane in the tropical heat. Working alongside these slaves, but for wages, were more than one hundred thousand Europeans who had come to Cuba to seek their fortunes.

A slave revolt in 1791 in neighboring Haiti prompted hundreds of sugarcane planters to migrate to Cuba. The more sugar they grew, the more the world wanted. By the middle of the nineteenth century, Cuba produced more sugar than any other place in the world. Planters built magnificent, castlelike homes, and cane fields stretched to the horizon. The first railroad in Cuba was built in 1837 to bring the sugar harvest to port.

An owner surveys his sugar plantation in southwestern Cuba in 1853.

Plantation owners in Cuba forced enslaved people to perform backbreaking tasks such as cutting and crushing sugarcane.

A number of American politicians and businessmen grew envious of the lucrative sugar business in Cuba. They wanted the island to be part of the United States. American slaveholders in particular were interested in Cuba. They believed that adding another territory where slavery was allowed would help them resist the growing movement in the United States to limit slavery. In 1848, U.S. president James K. Polk offered the amazing sum of US$100 million for Cuba. Spain turned him down.

The enslaved workers who were making the Spanish rich, meanwhile, spent their lives in poverty and misery. All slaves worked hard, but the sugar fields were particularly brutal. Once a slave began working in the sugar fields, he or she lived only an average of eight more years.

On February 15, 1898, an explosion sank the USS *Maine*. Nearly three-quarters of the ship's crew died.

Meanwhile, the *criollos*—Spanish people born in Cuba—were becoming tired of Spain's policies. They wanted more freedom and more say in how Cuba was governed. Some wanted to become completely independent. In 1868, Carlos Manuel de Céspedes, a plantation owner from eastern Cuba, launched an uprising. He called for an end to slavery and an end to Spanish rule. This was the beginning of the Ten Years' War.

Spain rushed one hundred thousand troops to the island. In the next decade, a quarter million people would die in the violence. Eventually, the war wound down, and the government finally outlawed slavery in 1886. But Cuba still was not free from Spanish rule.

Poet and journalist José Martí, a Cuban living in the United States, kept the idea of revolution alive. He returned to Cuba in 1895 and joined General Máximo Gómez y Báez and Colonel Antonio Maceo y Grajales to fight the Spaniards. Martí died early in this second war of independence. Over time, so did thousands of Cubans, including many whom Spanish soldiers put in concentration camps.

In 1898, the United States sent a battleship called the USS *Maine* to Havana to protect U.S. interests such as sugar companies and fruit importers. When the ship exploded in

U.S. troops invaded Guantánamo Bay in June 1898, during the Spanish-American War.

Havana's harbor, the United States blamed Spain and declared war. The brief war was popular with Americans, many of whom thought Cuba should be a part of the United States. By the end of the year, Spain surrendered. After almost four hundred years, Cubans were free of Spanish rule.

The United States maintained control of Cuba for nearly four years before granting the island its independence. But even after U.S. troops left the island, Cuba remained financially dependent on the United States because of the millions of U.S. dollars invested in the country.

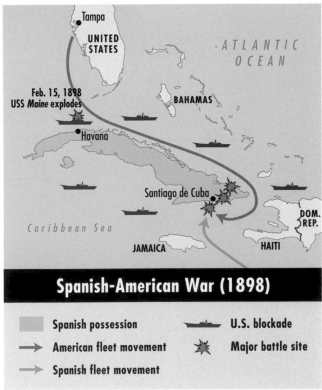

Spanish-American War (1898)

Tampa
UNITED STATES
ATLANTIC OCEAN
BAHAMAS
Feb. 15, 1898 USS *Maine* explodes
Havana
Santiago de Cuba
Caribbean Sea
JAMAICA
HAITI
DOM. REP.

- Spanish possession
- American fleet movement
- Spanish fleet movement
- U.S. blockade
- Major battle site

The early twentieth century was an exciting time for Cuba. The country grew wealthy as it exported vast amounts of sugar and other goods. The money was used to construct grand buildings and invest in education and the arts. Cuba became a popular tourist destination. Americans and Europeans traveled to Havana to enjoy its wide boulevards, warm weather, luxurious hotels, and festive nightspots.

But with prosperity came corruption. Government officials readily took bribes, and crime was common. Then, in 1929, the worldwide Great Depression hit, and sugar prices collapsed. People were thrown out of work. Many had nowhere to live and no food to eat. Some Cubans took to the streets demanding jobs. President Gerardo Machado responded violently. He ordered the police to arrest protesters and break up political meetings. Opposition to Machado grew, and he was forced from office in 1933.

He was replaced by a young reformer named Fulgencio Batista. For most of the next decade, Batista

President-elect Gerardo Machado tips his hat on the way to his inauguration in 1929.

Fulgencio Batista (right) meets with Earl E. T. Smith, the U.S. ambassador to Cuba, in July 1957.

served as head of the army rather than as president, but he always held the true power. During these years, the economy improved, democracy expanded as everyone gained the right to vote, and new laws protected workers' safety and limited the length of their workday.

Batista left office in 1944 and moved to Florida, apparently to retire. When he returned to Cuba in 1952 to run for president, it became apparent he was going to lose. With the backing of the military, he called off the elections and declared himself the head of government. Batista became a dictator. He lived lavishly, favoring wealthy American and organized-crime interests at the expense of his own people. As opposition to his regime grew, he rounded up opponents and sometimes had them killed.

Fidel Castro and Che Guevara (far right) led the rebellion to overthrow Fulgencio Batista.

A Young Rebel

A young lawyer was soon at the center of the resistance to Batista. Fidel Castro came from a rural, middle-class family. As part of the attempt to topple Batista in 1953, Castro led a group of revolutionaries in an attack on the Moncada army barracks. Castro was captured and sentenced to fifteen years in prison. Some of his fellow soldiers were tortured, which hardened public opinion against the Batista regime. Castro and his soldiers became heroes.

Castro served only two years in prison before Batista decided to free all political prisoners. Upon his release, Castro feared Batista would have him killed, so he fled to Mexico. There he rallied like-minded Cubans and an Argentine revolutionary named Ernesto "Che" Guevara de la Serna. They vowed to remove Batista. In November 1956, in a small, leaky boat named *Granma*, Castro and some eighty soldiers landed on a deserted beach in the south. The revolution had begun.

It did not start easily. Most of the revolutionaries were captured by Batista's troops. Castro, Guevara, and a few others headed into the hills. From there, they attacked police stations and army barracks. The government's troops fought badly or not at all.

Che Guevara, Revolutionary Hero

One of the most recognized Cuban revolutionaries around the world wasn't actually from Cuba. Ernesto "Che" Guevara de la Serna (1928–1967) was born to a middle-class family in Argentina. He trained to be a doctor and then decided to take a motorcycle trip across South America before settling down. The trip opened his eyes to the vast numbers of poor people and the corrupt governments all over the continent. Guevara resolved to do something.

In Mexico, Guevara joined Fidel Castro, who was there planning the Cuban Revolution. With Castro and eighty others, he sailed to Cuba on a leaky boat and took to the hills. Fearless in battle, Guevara led troops in decisive fighting at Santa Clara in December 1958.

When Castro took power, Guevara became an important part of the revolutionary government, but he was restless. He soon went to the African nation of Congo to train antigovernment troops and then to South America to start revolutions. Things went awry in Bolivia. Guevara and his men were ambushed, and he was killed.

From the time the Cuban Revolution triumphed, Guevara's likeness—a bearded face under a beret with a five-pointed star—has appeared on posters and T-shirts all over the world. To many people, he represents the ideal of a person who cares nothing for power or riches but instead wants justice for everyday people. Che Guevara remains a martyr and a hero in much of the world.

For the next two years, protests against Batista grew while the rebels battled government troops. The rebels took the city of Santa Clara in central Cuba in December 1958 and then entered Havana on December 30. Batista fled the country the next day. Castro and his supporters led a triumphant parade across Cuba, entering Havana on January 8, 1959. The people gave him a hero's welcome. Clearly, they supported the revolutionaries.

Rising Tensions

Castro's government immediately began reforming the economy. The government seized property and broke up large landholdings, or privately owned properties. U.S. companies owned a great deal of Cuba's land and many factories. Before the revolution, U.S. businesses owned 75 percent of the agricultural land in Cuba and 40 percent of the sugar industry. These companies resented losing their property. By May 1959, Castro had divided large plantations into small parcels for average people. He also became friendly with the Soviet Union, which at the

In 1955, a Cuban worker cans peanut oil at a factory once owned by the Hershey Company. Hershey owned several factories and plantations in Cuba in the first half of the twentieth century.

time was the world's largest communist nation and the United States' main adversary. (The Soviet Union has since broken apart into Russia and fourteen smaller nations.)

Many Cubans who had supported the revolution disliked the direction Castro was taking the country. In the first three years after the revolution, an estimated two hundred thousand Cubans fled the country. Most of those who left had professional jobs or belonged to Cuba's middle class. Many ended up in Florida. Some of these former Cubans living in Florida took part in an invasion of Cuba on April 17, 1961, at a place called the Bay of Pigs. They were quickly captured.

Guards watch a group of men captured following the failed Bay of Pigs invasion in 1961.

The Bay of Pigs Invasion

Just months after Castro took power in 1959, the U.S. government began to plan his overthrow. The United States rallied anti-Castro Cubans in Florida and elsewhere. The Central Intelligence Agency (CIA), the government agency in charge of gathering information about foreign countries, trained fifteen hundred Cubans living in the United States in military tactics and planned an invasion.

In April 1961, the anti-Castro force landed at the Bay of Pigs in southern Cuba. The CIA had convinced the invaders that the people of Cuba would welcome them. But Castro was ready for the invasion. He detained thousands of people he thought might join the raiders, and he encouraged police and military forces to fight the invaders. As a result, about one thousand of the about fifteen hundred were captured. The Cuban army performed well, showing bravery and discipline.

The failed invasion embarrassed the United States and infuriated Castro. The Cubans' triumph over the invaders made him even more popular.

Relations between the United States and Cuba turned tense. As the Cuban government continued to take over U.S.-owned companies in Cuba, the United States began a trade embargo, which stopped trade between the two countries.

In 1962, the Soviets provided a worried Castro with missiles. At the time, the United States and the Soviet Union were in the middle of the cold war, in which they were competing for influence around the world. President John F. Kennedy did not want Soviet missiles so close to the United States, so he ordered a naval blockade around the island to prevent ships from delivering more Soviet missiles to Cuba. According to some reports, Castro asked the Soviets to fire missiles at the U.S. mainland. After several days during which the countries' leaders considered the possibility of nuclear war, the Soviets agreed to remove the missiles if the United States would pledge not to invade Cuba. The crisis passed, and a "hot war" (one that includes the firing of weapons) was averted.

The Face of Cuba

Fidel Castro was the long-time face of Cuba. Admired by some and despised by others, he will go down in history as a patriot, a dictator, and a revolutionary.

Castro's early years were calm. He was born in eastern Cuba in 1926, the son of a prosperous sugarcane farmer. Castro did well in school and, like so many Cuban boys, learned to love baseball.

He began studying law at the University of Havana in 1945. In college, he criticized the corruption of the Cuban government. A talented and charismatic speaker, Castro drew the attention of those around him. He soon joined the antigovernment Partido Ortodoxo (Orthodox Party). This party opposed corruption and proposed major reforms. Many of its members wanted the government to redistribute land, taking it from wealthy owners and giving it to the poor.

The future dictator married, graduated from law school in 1950, and ran for the Cuban parliament in 1952. But that year, Fulgencio Batista seized power and canceled the elections. This only made Castro more determined to fight the government. The following year, he began his efforts to overthrow Batista. He attacked a military barracks, was imprisoned and then freed, and fled to Mexico. He returned to Cuba in 1956 prepared to battle the government. By January 1959, Castro was in control of Cuba.

Relations with the United States and the Soviet Union dominated Castro's decades in power. He was at first popular in the United States, but as the Cuban government seized American-owned land and businesses, the U.S. government turned against him. Castro

soon gained the friendship of the Soviet Union, which poured money into Cuba until its demise in 1991.

Over the years, Castro saw Cuba through good times and bad. He marked each patriotic holiday with lengthy, dramatic speeches that often criticized the United States. Cubans did not always love Castro, but their support for him increased whenever they saw the United States attack his government, either in words or in actions. Castro stepped down as president of Cuba in 2008, after forty-nine years in power.

The unfinished roads and sidewalks in the mining town of Moa highlight some of the problems with the country's infrastructure.

Meanwhile, more changes were sweeping the island. Rural peasants got lessons in reading and writing, and new schools opened. Money from the Soviet Union greatly improved health care. But at the same time, city infrastructures—their buildings, streets, and other physical things citizens rely on—crumbled, and the sugarcane crop decreased in size.

Some goods in short supply were rationed by the government. That is, Cuban families by law could only get small amounts of items such as meat, rice, bread, milk, toilet paper, and fuel oil. Each family had a ration book in which they kept track of how much the government allowed them to get. No one starved, but much of Cuban society felt discontent.

Growth and Change

In the 1960s and 1970s, Cuba tried to promote revolution in other countries around the world. In 1975, Cuba sent troops to the African nation of Angola. Nearly three hundred thousand Cuban troops fought in Angola between 1975 and 1989.

The 1970s were a time of economic growth in Cuba. The basic conditions of people's lives began to improve. But the country also relied more and more on the Soviet Union. By

1988, 87 percent of Cuban trade was with the Soviet Union or other countries that the Soviet Union dominated. When the Soviet Union fell apart in 1991, Cubans found that they missed the millions of dollars' worth of aid the Soviets had provided for years.

A period of great need hit Cuba. The country suffered desperate food shortages, and majestic buildings fell into further disrepair. The stream of Cubans leaving for the United States continued. Many Cubans who reached the United States sent money back home to help their relatives survive.

By 1993, Cuban officials had changed the rules governing the economy so that some private businesses could flourish. Farmers could sell their produce at farmers' markets, and other people were allowed to start their own small businesses. The government also legalized the use of U.S. dollars. Gradually, the economy recovered.

In 2006, Fidel Castro became too ill to perform his duties as president. His brother Raúl took over on a temporary basis and then became president in 2008. With the change in leadership came a chance for relations between Cuba and the United States to improve. Only time will tell whether that comes to pass.

Cubans crowd a homemade raft as they attempt to flee to the United States.

A Communist Nation

CHAPTER

FIVE

IN THE TWENTIETH CENTURY, MANY COUNTRIES AROUND the world had communist governments. Today, Cuba is one of the few communist countries that remain. Others include China, Laos, and North Korea. Cuba's 1976 constitution outlines its communist system of government.

Under communism, the government controls the economy and owns all the businesses. In most communist nations, a few powerful people run the country. For most of his forty-nine-year rule, Fidel Castro held the titles of president of the republic, first secretary of the Cuban Communist Party (in Spanish, Partido Comunista de Cuba, or PCC), president of the Council of State, and president of the Council of Ministers.

Opposite: **Construction on the Cuban capitol began in 1926. After it was completed, the building housed the national government until Fidel Castro came into power.**

The Cuban Flag

The Cuban flag is made up of five horizontal stripes of alternating blue and white. On the left side of the

flag is a red triangle with a white, five-pointed star in the center. The flag was first flown in 1850 in the city of Cárdenas by Cubans opposed to Spanish rule. The blue stripes represent the departments into which the island was divided at the time, while the white stripes stand for the purity of independence. The red of the triangle symbolizes the blood shed by revolutionaries, and the white star represents liberty.

The Cuban Communist Party, with some six hundred thousand members, is the only political party allowed in Cuba. It is the country's most powerful organization. All members of the National Assembly of People's Power, the nation's congress, belong to the PCC. Mayors, chiefs of police, and other government officials are also party members. The PCC is everywhere in Cuba. The party manages sports teams, organizes hurricane safety, supervises health care, manages education, and conducts elections.

Those who belong to the PCC get real advantages. Goods that are rationed for average people are available to party members and their families. Cuba is filled with rickety old cars, but party members often drive newer models. PCC

A meeting of the National Assembly of People's Power in Havana. All members of the National Assembly belong to the PCC.

The New President

Throughout Fidel Castro's life, his younger brother Raúl was always at his side. When Fidel led an attack on the Moncada army barracks, Raúl was with him. They were both sent to prison for the attack, and both went to Mexico after their release. Together, they sailed on a rickety ship back to Cuba in 1956 to start the Cuban Revolution.

After their revolution succeeded, Raúl became his brother's right-hand man, his chief aide. When Cuba's new constitution went into effect in 1976, Raúl took the title of first vice president. In 2006, when Fidel became too ill to function as president, Raúl took over. In 2008, the National Assembly officially elected him president.

Although Raúl and Fidel Castro are brothers and have worked side by side their entire lives, they are very different. Fidel was a charismatic leader. Raúl is quiet and businesslike.

No one knows the direction Raúl Castro will take the country. Many people credit him with convincing

Fidel to allow farmers to sell their own produce when the country suffered economic troubles in the 1990s. This has led some to believe that Raúl might be open to change. But many others believe he is unwavering in his commitment to communism.

members are also allowed much more freedom of movement than are average citizens.

Every five years, the PCC holds a congress during which ordinary citizens can present their views. This congress elects a Central Committee of 150 members, which oversees the work of the party. The Central Committee elects a Politburo of 25 people, which enforces communist policy. Fidel Castro headed the Politburo before he became ill. Now, Raúl Castro runs the Politburo.

NATIONAL GOVERNMENT OF CUBA

Executive Branch

PRESIDENT

VICE PRESIDENTS

COUNCIL OF MINISTERS

COUNCIL OF STATE

Legislative Branch

NATIONAL ASSEMBLY OF
PEOPLE'S POWER

Judicial Branch

PEOPLE'S SUPREME COURT

REGIONAL COURTS

The National Government

The president is the head of the government in Cuba. The National Assembly elects the president every four years. Two groups advise the president. One is the Council of Ministers, which is made up of five vice presidents and the heads of all the executive-branch ministries, such as the Ministry of Justice and the Ministry of Foreign Affairs. The other is the thirty-one-member Council of State, which also includes the vice presidents along with important members of the PCC. The Council of State has legislative power when the National Assembly is not in session.

The National Assembly of People's Power has 614 members. Members of the National Assembly stand for election every five years, but the elections are not contested. The only person running in each district is the PCC candidate. All people sixteen years of age or older, whether party members or not, can vote in Cuba.

The National Assembly passes new laws and has the power to change the constitution. In reality, the National Assembly has little to do with making laws. It has never failed to pass a law proposed by the government. Presidential decrees are enforced as law even before the National Assembly approves them. And when the National Assembly is not in session—

which is for much of the year—the Council of State has legislative power. To Cuba's leaders, the National Assembly is not so much a lawmaking body as a source of ideas to better the country and a way for representatives to relay what the people in their home areas may be doing and feeling.

Courts make up the judicial branch of government. Cuba's highest court is the People's Supreme Court. The National Assembly elects judges to this court. Cuba also has seven regional courts.

Family members of Cuban dissidents on trial wait outside a court building in Havana.

Cuba's judicial system differs from those in the United States and Canada in some important ways. No U.S. or Canadian citizen can be held indefinitely without being charged. But Cubans, especially those who oppose the government, can be imprisoned for years for no reason.

Stifling Opposition

Since Fidel Castro took control of Cuba in 1959, hundreds of thousands of Cubans have fled the country. Many crossed the rough seas to Florida in small boats.

Some people who oppose the government remain in Cuba, but they are not allowed to speak out. Dissent is not allowed in Cuba. Average citizens spy on their neighbors as members of the Committee for the Defense of the Revolution. Courts prosecute people accused of anticommunist activity, and prison terms for dissenters are common. Dissenters also may be judged insane and put in mental institutions. Because the government controls most work, dissenters can also lose their jobs.

Huber Matos, once a member of Castro's rebel forces, later opposed Castro's government. Matos was convicted of treason and spent twenty years in prison.

In recent years, the treatment of dissenters has relaxed somewhat. Dissenters today are as often shunned as prosecuted, and visitors to the island see little tension among the nation's citizens.

The Military

All Cubans, both male and female, must serve in the military for two years at some time between the ages of seventeen and twenty-eight. Often, more Cubans reach the age of military service than are needed in the army. During these times, Cubans perform their national service working on government farm and construction projects rather than in uniform.

Members of the Cuban military wave flags during a ceremony in 1976.

The National Anthem

The Cuban national anthem was composed in 1867 by Pedro Figueredo, a lawyer and musician who lived in the city of Bayamo, in eastern Cuba. Figueredo wrote "La Bayamesa" ("The Bayamo Song"), as the anthem is known, a year before the start of the brutal Ten Years' War. Figueredo was killed by Spanish forces during the war. After Cuba became independent, his song became the national anthem.

Spanish lyrics

Al combate corred bayomesas, que la patria os contempla orgullosa!

No temáis una muerte gloriosa, que morir por la patria es vivir.

En cadenas vivir, es vivir en afrenta y oprobio sumido,

Del clarín escuchad el sonido, A las armas valientes, corred!

English translation

Run to the fight Bayomeses, for the fatherland is watching you proudly!

Do not fear a glorious death, for to die for the fatherland is to live.

To live in chains is to live in dishonor and ignominy,

From the clarion hear the sound, To the weapons, valiant warriors, run!

Havana: Did You Know This?

Havana is the largest city in Cuba, with a population of 2,686,000. It is the industrial and intellectual heart of Cuba as well as being the capital. It is also Cuba's most important port. The city is filled with factories, warehouses, stately theaters, and magnificent museums.

Havana at one time was the most popular destination in the Caribbean. It had great music, great food, handsome buildings, a mix of people, and a welcoming ocean nearby. Decades of neglect have left the city rundown. Hundreds of homes built for people who

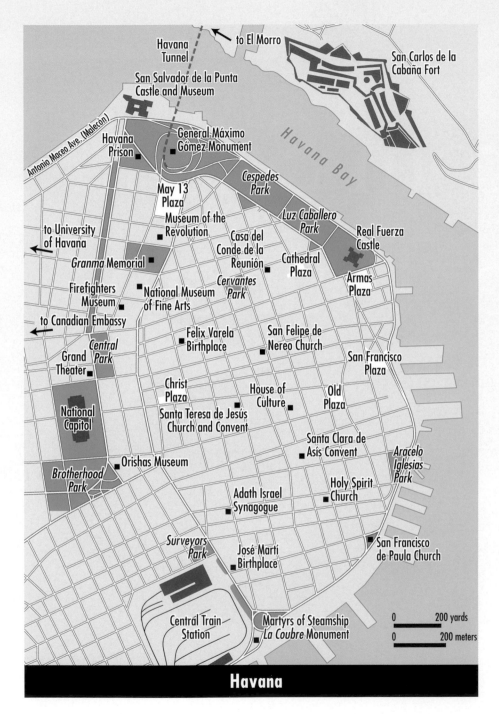

became wealthy in the sugar industry still stand, but many of them have been carved up into apartments. Paint peels from walls, and mildew grows on the sides of many buildings.

Havana's crumbling buildings still attract tourists from Canada and Europe. Other city highlights include the Malecón, a romantic seawall and walkway that separates city and ocean, and the old Spanish fort El Morro, which guards the harbor entrance.

From Sugar to Tourism

Fields of sugarcane cover much of the island. Sugar has been the country's main agricultural product for hundreds of years.

FOR MUCH OF CUBAN HISTORY, MOST PEOPLE WORKED IN agriculture. Every year, thousands of Cubans would head for the sugarcane fields with big knives called machetes. The workers would chop the cane so that it could be processed into sugar. Nowadays, machines harvest most of the cane, and only 20 percent of Cubans work in agriculture.

Today, most Cubans—about 61 percent—work in the service sector, the part of the economy in which people earn money for what they do, not what they make. Waiters, cab drivers, teachers, truckers, launderers, doctors, nurses, and others make up the bulk of Cuba's economy. Another 19 percent of Cubans work in industrial jobs. They may pour steel, make cement, or build houses.

Opposite: **Coffee pickers in the Escambray Mountains take a break.**

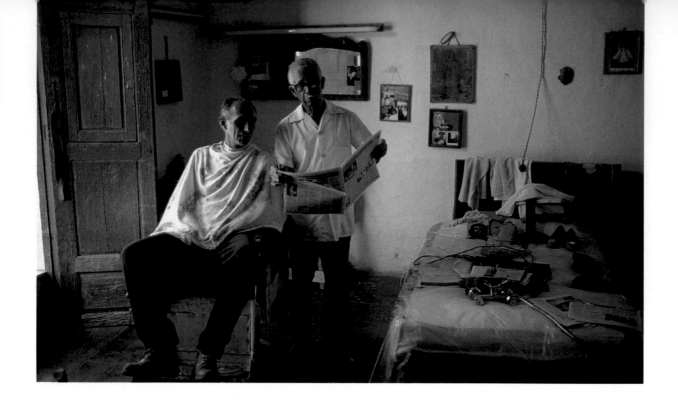

A barber in Trinidad looks at the newspaper with a customer. Barbers are part of the service industry.

In addition, the Cuban government requires all Cubans to perform 150 hours of volunteer work per year. Cubans work on government projects such as construction, harvesting crops, paving highways, cutting back vegetation, loading trucks, and more. Because citizens usually have no experience doing these jobs, the work they do is sometimes of poor quality.

At one time, the Cuban government employed more than 90 percent of the nation's workforce. People worked at farms and factories and schools run by the government. But in recent years, Cuba has allowed some people to go into business for themselves. People might run their own small restaurant or other family business. Others work for themselves without government permission. Today, the Cuban government employs about 75 percent of the country's workers, according to some estimates.

No matter what Cubans do for a living, paychecks are small. Even doctors and lawyers are paid modestly. Many Cubans work more than one job to survive. It is not unusual to meet, for example, a well-educated chemist who also drives an old cab in her spare time.

Service Industries

Service industries make up the largest part of Cuba's economy, and among those industries, tourism provides a bright spot in Cuba's economy. More than two million foreign tourists travel to Cuba every year, spending more than US$2 billion. The

Money Facts

Cuba uses two types of currency: pesos and convertible pesos. People use pesos to buy everyday goods such as groceries. They spend convertible pesos at hotels, many restaurants, museums, and other places that cater to tourists. Cubans receive part of their wages in pesos and part in convertible pesos. In theory, tourists are supposed to use only convertible pesos. In 2008, US$1 equaled 23 pesos, and 1 peso equaled US$0.04. One convertible peso equals about 24 pesos and US$1.08.

Both kinds of pesos are divided into 100 centavos. Each has paper money in values of 1, 3, 5, 10, 20, 50, and 100 pesos. For normal pesos, coins come in values of 1, 5, and 20 centavos and 1 and 3 pesos. For convertible pesos, coins come in values of 1, 5, 10, 25, and 50 centavos and 1 peso.

The front of normal pesos depicts heroes from Cuban history. For example, the 3-peso note carries a portrait of Che Guevara. On the back is an image of Guevara cutting sugarcane. Convertible pesos depict monuments to Cuban heroes.

United States, however, does not allow most of its citizens to travel to Cuba. This travel ban is part of the U.S. economic embargo against Cuba.

The droves of Europeans and Canadians who visit Cuba every winter enjoy its warm water, romantic cities, and friendly people. Several European companies have built grand new hotels and resorts there, and Havana and other cities have many fancy restaurants that cater to foreigners. These places are off limits to most Cubans, who cannot afford them.

Many international travelers enjoy Cuba's upscale resorts and hotels. The Hotel Nacional de Cuba, shown here, opened in 1930.

A worker stacks sacks of sugar at a sugar mill in Mantanzas.

Manufacturing

Sugar is Cuba's leading manufactured product. More than one hundred sugar mills make refined sugar from Cuban-grown sugarcane. But Cuba's sugar industry is in decline. In 2002, the country produced about 3.5 million metric tons of refined sugar, less than half the amount it produced in 1990.

Cigars, oil, food products, cement products, and textiles are other leading manufactured goods. A dozen factories in Cuba produce rum, an alcoholic drink made from sugarcane juice.

What Cuba Grows, Makes, and Mines

Agriculture (2000)

Sugarcane	36,000,000 metric tons
Oranges	441,000 metric tons
Rice	369,000 metric tons

Manufacturing

Sugar (2002)	3,522,000 metric tons
Cement (2000)	1,633,000 metric tons
Cigars (2005)	160,000,000 units

Mining

Nickel (2007)	76,000 metric tons
Chromite (2004)	34,000 metric tons

Fishers drag a net onto a dock on Cayo Largo, an island south of the mainland.

The production of medicines is a growing industry in Cuba. Vaccines produced in Cuba sell in many parts of the world. Cuba has a state-of-the-art lab where scientists develop new medicines and therapies.

Agriculture and Mining

Cuba was once the world's leading sugar producer. This is no longer true, but sugarcane remains the county's top agricultural product. Cuba also produces tobacco, coffee, rice, and citrus fruits such as oranges. Fishing is a growing industry in Cuba. The country exports shrimp, red snapper, and tuna.

Cuba has the third-largest reserves of nickel in the world. Large amounts of chromite and cobalt are also found in the country.

The U.S. Trade Embargo

Nothing has affected Cuba like the embargo the United States placed against it in 1960. The United States began the embargo because it wanted to punish the Cuban government for taking over land and businesses owned by Americans. The U.S. government hoped to change Cuba's political system, forcing it away from communism.

The embargo initially banned all trade between the two countries except for food and medicine. Soon, the U.S. Congress voted for a total embargo of trade with Cuba. U.S. citizens were also banned from traveling to Cuba.

The government of Cuba was less than two years old when the embargo began. Fidel Castro feared that it would damage the Cuban economy, and he was right. Most cars and many industrial machines depended on parts and equipment from the United States. Without them, the machines broke down. The embargo made it difficult to repair trains, buses, passenger cars, tractors, and many other machines. All kinds of businesses suffered, and many people lost their jobs.

Resources

Forests	Au	Gold	Fz Fertilizer
Fruit and vegetables	Cem	Cement	Mn Manganese
Livestock	Co	Cobalt	Ni Nickel
Tobacco	Cr	Chromite	Oil
Tropical crops	Cu	Copper	W Tungsten
Nonagricultural land	Fe	Iron	Zn Zinc

In 2002, former president Jimmy Carter (left) became the first U.S. president to visit Cuba since the revolution.

In the 1970s, President Jimmy Carter loosened the embargo a bit and lifted the travel ban so that Americans could again visit Cuba. But in the 1980s, President Ronald Reagan reversed those changes.

In 1992, Cuba asked the United Nations (UN) to help end the embargo. Most of the world's countries belong to the United Nations, an organization dedicated to solving conflicts among nations peacefully. The UN voted 88–4 to ask the United States to drop the embargo, with the United States being one of the four countries voting no. Virtually every year after that, the UN voted overwhelmingly that the embargo should be dropped, but the United States has refused.

Meanwhile, many visitors to Cuba say they can see the damage the embargo has caused. Buildings are in disrepair. Despite recent good harvests, some people in Cuba go to bed hungry. Power outages are common because electrical-supply equipment is old. And the entire transit system is patched together haphazardly.

Many Cuban Americans support the embargo. They despise the Castro regime, feeling that it ruined their country. Even though many of them have relatives suffering in Cuba, they believe that the embargo will ultimately drive communism out of Cuba. Although the embargo has been effect for decades, it has not yet accomplished that goal.

Foreign Trade

Although the United States refuses to do business with Cuba, the country has many other trade partners. Cuba exports goods to countries such as the Netherlands, Canada, China, and Spain. Cuba's top exports include sugar, nickel, tobacco, fish, medical products, and citrus fruits.

Goods arrive in Cuba from Venezuela, China, Spain, Germany, and Canada. Major imported items include oil, food, machinery, and chemicals. Some of the chemicals Cuba imports go into making the medicine it exports.

In recent years, Cuba and the oil-rich nation of Venezuela have become major trading partners. Since 2000, Cuba has been able to purchase 98,000 barrels of oil per day from Venezuela at low prices. Cuba found a clever way to pay for the Venezuelan oil. Cuba has many doctors and nurses, so the country pays for oil products in part by lending Cuban medical professionals to Venezuela. Many more poor people in Venezuela now have quality medical care, and Cuba has fuel for its vehicles.

Oil storage tanks in Havana. A conflict in Venezuela in 2003 slowed the number of tankers delivering oil to Cuba.

The Cuban People

MOST CUBANS HAVE A MIXED ANCESTRY. MANY Cubans can trace their roots to a mix of Spanish and Indian ancestors. Spaniards continued to immigrate to Cuba until the early twentieth century. As late as the nineteenth century, scientists say, the majority of people in Cuba who called themselves Spanish had one or more Taíno ancestors.

Opposite: **A mother and her daughters in Havana. Most families in Cuba have one or two children.**

An estimated 19 percent of Cuba's population is under the age of fifteen.

Ethnic Cuba

Mixed	58%
White	28%
Black	12%
Other	2%

Enslaved laborers harvest tobacco on a Cuban plantation in the nineteenth century. Spain did not outlaw slavery in Cuba until 1886.

Beginning in the sixteenth century, large numbers of enslaved Africans were also brought to the island. Those who survived the terrifying voyage to the Western Hemisphere were put to work in sugarcane fields or performing other agricultural labor. An estimated half million Africans were brought to Cuba from the 1500s until 1886, when slavery was abolished on the island. Today, about 58 percent of Cubans are of mixed African and European ancestry.

In the nineteenth century, many French people arrived on the island from neighboring Haiti. They became part of the

Cuba has a large Chinese population. A Chinese newspaper, *Kwong Wah Po*, is printed on a one-hundred-year old press (above) in Havana's Chinatown.

Cuban elite. People from the Canary Islands, Spanish possessions off the west coast of Spain, also came to Cuba. They arrived seeking better lives and often worked for pay, alongside slaves, in the fields. People of African descent from places like Haiti and Jamaica also migrated to Cuba and mixed into the population.

Some Cubans have an Asian background. An estimated 150,000 Chinese people moved to Cuba, mostly in the nineteenth century. They left China seeking more opportunity, and many ended up working in mines.

Students in Cienfuegos walk home after school. Students of different grade levels wear different color uniforms.

Cuba is also home to a few thousand Europeans from the former Soviet Union, along with people who trace their ancestry to Portugal, Italy, or other European countries. Since the revolution, some people have moved to Cuba from various South and Central American countries. Most of these new-comers sympathized with the goals of Fidel Castro and the revolution.

The Cuban government has worked to make Cuba into a colorless society. It passed laws making discrimination illegal. In fact, racial distinctions have shrunk since the revolution. Still, managers and supervisors are more likely to be white. The government itself is mostly composed of white men at the upper levels.

More than a million people have left Cuba since the revolution. At first, most of those leaving were white and middle class or wealthy. They were dissatisfied with Castro's new policies. Today, the people who flee Cuba come from all backgrounds. They are searching for better jobs, greater political or social freedom, and greater economic opportunity.

Cubans often leave the island on a rickety raft or in a homemade boat. Their trip to Florida means a dangerous voyage across high seas, sometimes in rough weather. Over the years, thousands of people trying to leave Cuba have died. They are also in danger because the Cuban navy sometimes uses force to stop people from leaving. The people fleeing

Cuba do not have permission to enter the United States. If the U.S. Coast Guard stops a boat before it lands in the United States, the U.S. government sends the people on the boat back to Cuba, where they are sometimes jailed. If a boat makes it to the Florida coast, the people on board are permitted to stay and begin the process of becoming legal U.S. residents.

Cubans head toward the United States in a boat made from a truck. The U.S. Coast Guard stopped them 40 miles (65 km) from Florida and sent them back to Cuba.

Some Cubans also try to reach the United States through Mexico. They fly or take a boat to Mexico and then head overland into the United States. Others buy fake documents and fly directly to Miami, Florida, or elsewhere. Some Cubans and Americans take advantage of the desperate people trying to reach the United States. Although they say they will help the Cubans enter the United States, instead all they do is take the fleeing people's money and valuables. Both the United States and Cuba prosecute people who make money transporting desperate migrants.

Cubans who reach Florida join the large Cuban community already there. But they inevitably leave behind friends

Cuban immigrants in the Little Havana neighborhood in Miami, Florida, play dominoes in a park behind a bust of Máximo Gómez y Báez. Gómez was a military commander in the Ten Years' War.

and relatives whom they will probably never see again. Many of those who immigrate to the United States send money back home to their relatives still in Cuba.

City and Country

Cuba is home to more than eleven million people. About 75 percent of Cubans live in cities, and more rural Cubans would move to urban areas if the government permitted them to. No one is allowed to move to Havana without permission. The government believes that if too many people moved to the city, services would be overwhelmed and there would be not be enough jobs to go around. In some ways, life is more difficult in Havana than in rural areas. For example, city dwellers, unlike their country cousins, can't easily grow food to add to the rationed amount they may buy. Many Cubans also live in the small towns that pepper the countryside.

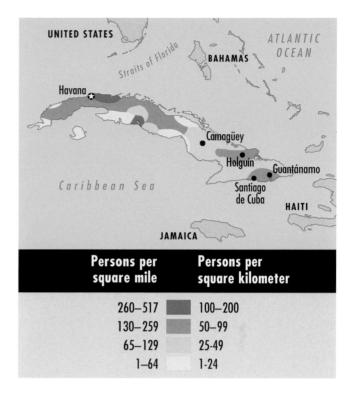

Persons per square mile	Persons per square kilometer
260–517	100–200
130–259	50–99
65–129	25-49
1–64	1-24

Work and Family

After the revolution, new laws stated that husbands had to share housework with their wives. The reality, however, is quite different. Women continue to do most of the work around the home. At the same time, many women have

Cuba's Largest Cities

Havana	2,686,000
Santiago de Cuba	554,400
Camagüey	354,400
Holguín	319,300
Guantánamo	274,300

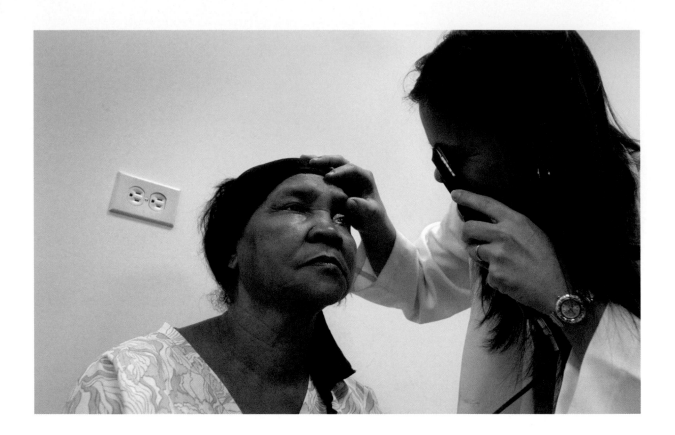

A doctor checks a woman's eyes at a hospital in Havana. About half of the doctors in Cuba are women.

entered the workforce. Many hold professional positions, working as doctors, lawyers, and scientists. In fact, women hold about two-thirds of all professional and technical jobs in Cuba. One field in which women have not made much headway is politics. Men hold almost all high-level political jobs.

Cuba has a high divorce rate. More than half the people over age twenty-five have been divorced. Cuba also has one of the lowest birthrates in the Western Hemisphere. The average Cuban woman has only 1.4 children, down from an average of 3.2 children in 1970. Cuba helps working mothers. Women get one year of maternity leave and free day care. It is common for children, parents, and grandparents to live in the same house, so babysitters are often readily available.

Speaking Spanish

Spanish is the official language of Cuba. Words from the Taíno language and various African languages have enriched the Spanish language. Taíno words adopted by the Spanish include *barbacoa* (barbecue), *canoa* (canoe), *huracán* (hurricane), *hamaca* (hammock), *patata* (potato), and *tabaco* (tobacco). English is now the most commonly studied foreign language in school.

Common Spanish Words and Phrases

sí	yes
no	no
¿Cómo está usted?	How are you?
por favor	please
gracias	thank you
de nada	it's nothing; you're welcome
buenos días	good day; hello
adios	good-bye
hoy	today
mañana	tomorrow
¿Cuánto cuesta?	What does it cost?
¿Dónde está . . . ?	Where is . . . ?

Several newspapers are published in Cuba. Here, a vendor at a tourist's fair in Havana hands out copies of the international version of *Granma*, the daily newspaper of the Cuban Communist Party.

Spiritual Life

In 1997, Cuba's Cardinal Jaime Ortega led the country's first outdoor mass in more than thirty years.

THE SPANISH BROUGHT ROMAN CATHOLICISM TO CUBA in the 1500s. Today, it is the nation's largest religion. Approximately 70 percent of the people of Cuba are Roman Catholic. Other religions also flourish in Cuba. Some Cubans of African descent practice the religions of their ancestors, while a variety of Protestant groups hold services. Many Cubans, however, say that their lives are free of religion.

Roman Catholicism

Roman Catholics in Cuba hold the same beliefs as Roman Catholics everywhere. They believe that Jesus Christ is the son

Opposite: **Havana's Church of Santo Angel Custodio was built in the seventeenth century. It was rebuilt and enlarged in the 1800s after a hurricane destroyed much of it.**

Frei Betto speaks in 2008 during a ceremony honoring Fidel Castro.

of God, sent to earth to die for the sins of human beings. Catholics also believe that if they are in a state of grace when they die, then their sins will be forgiven and they can enter into heaven.

After the Cuban Revolution, the government tried to steer people away from religion. Some Catholic officials were forced to leave the country, and few practicing Catholics were given good jobs. Cuban officials even imprisoned some people who opposed government policy on religion.

Then, in the 1980s, Fidel Castro began to show signs of being more open to religion. He and a Brazilian priest named Carlos Alberto Libânio Christo, better known as Frei Betto, engaged in a thoughtful dialogue about religion. Castro and Frei Betto agreed in their support of liberation theology, the idea that the church must defend and pay special

The President and the Priest

In 1985, Frei Betto, a Brazilian priest, talked with Cuban president Fidel Castro for many hours about religion. These conversations resulted in a book entitled *Fidel and Religion*. The volume records twenty-three hours of interviews between the president and the priest. During the interviews, Castro told Frei Betto that he resented "the church of the conquistadores" but greatly admired oppressed Christians. He said he wondered why the church never condemned slavery or the stealing of land from native peoples.

Castro also explained that he believed that early Christians would have supported liberation theology. He described early Christianity as "Christianity at its best, at its most beautiful and attractive." He admired early Christians in part because their persecution by the Romans made them stronger.

attention to the poor and the oppressed. Meanwhile, the Soviet Union, which was influential in Cuba and opposed religion, was weakening. When the Soviet Union fell apart, Cuba's economy suffered. Some people turned to their faith during the hard times that followed.

In 1998, Pope John Paul II, then the head of the Roman Catholic Church, paid a visit to Cuba at Castro's request. The people of Cuba received him warmly. After the pope's visit, the government became more tolerant of religion. Churches that had fallen into disrepair after the revolution were spruced up. Christmas again became an official public holiday.

The Pope in Cuba

Pope John Paul II paid his only visit to Cuba in 1998. The visit surprised some people because he was strongly anticommunist. John Paul II was Polish, and for much of his adult life, Poland was under a communist government. The pope and the Polish government were often at odds, and he backed protesters who fought to end communism in Poland.

While in Cuba, John Paul II talked with students at the University of Havana, visited a medical center, and met President Fidel Castro as well as religious leaders. The government allowed workers time off to attend religious events during the pope's visit. His visit signaled that the government's attitude toward Roman Catholicism and religion in general was warming. After years of hardship, religious people were again allowed to worship as they saw fit.

Religions of Cuba	
Roman Catholicism	70%
Santería	13%
Protestantism	3%
Other African religions	3%
No religion	10%

Most Catholics in Cuba do not attend regular church services. Instead, they practice their beliefs in the privacy of their homes. The biggest religious holiday in Cuba is Christmas—which celebrates the birth of Jesus Christ—on December 25. Cubans also hold a religious parade on December 17 called the Procession of the Miracles.

A child plays with ornaments on his family's Christmas tree in Havana in 2007. Cuba has become more open to religion in recent years, and Christmas has again become popular.

A Santería ritual called *rogación de cabeza* ("cleansing of the head") is performed in Santiago. It includes prayers and applying a coconut paste to the head.

Santería

The most common African-influenced religion is Santería, a blend of Roman Catholicism and the religion of the Yoruba people of West Africa. Enslaved Yorubans who were taken to Cuba brought their religion with them.

Santería features priests called *babalaos*, who help believers get in touch with the spirit world. Festivals featuring music, dancing, and occasionally animal sacrifice are an important part of the religion.

The religion is populated with saints, called *orishas*, many of whom have a Christian origin. One of the most popular, for example, is Lazarus, a biblical figure who represents Cuba's poor. Saints are thought to play a role in the destiny of each believer.

A Santería priest sits in front of an altar at a museum dedicated to Santería in Madruga.

Santería altars are common in homes and on the streets of Cuban cities. They sometimes include dolls, bits of food, Christian symbols, candles, photos, flowers, small statues, or mementos of people who have recently died. People of all faiths—or no faith—respect Santería shrines. These shrines are the center of religious life for many Cubans of African descent, who offer daily prayers to the saints. A popular figure on family altars is Santa Bárbara, who is also the African *orisha* known as Changó. The Havana suburb of Guanabacoa is home to large numbers of people who practice Santería.

Today, about three hundred thousand Cubans practice various forms of Protestant Christianity. There are Baptists, Methodists, Presbyterians, and many other groups. Evangelical Protestants, who teach a strict code of behavior, have the fastest-growing religious groups in Cuba today. The growing groups include the Assemblies of God and Pentecostals.

Members of a Protestant Bible-study group sing during a meeting in Havana.

Cuba is also home to a small Jewish community. Many Jews came to Cuba in the early twentieth century. By 1924, Cuba had a Jewish population of more than twenty thousand. Their numbers have been dwindling ever since. Today, there are an estimated 1,500 Jewish Cubans. Most live in Havana. Cuba also has small Muslim and Baha'i communities.

The grand rabbi of Israel, Israel Meir Lau, visited the Jewish cemetery in Havana on a trip to Cuba in 1994.

A Cuban man listens to the radio. Radio broadcasts provide Cubans with news, religious broadcasts, and music from around the world.

Religion in Practice

People of all faiths can be more open about their religion today than they were in the early decades following the revolution. During the early Castro years, they had to register their religion with the government. This may have frightened some Protestants, because they are in the minority. Nowadays, Cubans openly listen to religious broadcasts beaming out from Florida and elsewhere. They no longer feel the need to conceal their faith.

A Cultural Medley

CUBANS LOVE MUSIC. WHY ELSE WOULD SUCH A SMALL place have more than 220 radio stations? If a home has electricity, it has a radio. All varieties of Cuban music spring from those radios, including traditional forms such as *son* and *guajira*. Salsa, African, rap, rock, reggae, and many other kinds of music are also popular in Cuba.

The Music of Cuba

How can one island produce so much good music? Part of the answer is the rich mix of Spanish and African cultures. This

Two men play horns on the Malecón in Havana.

is particularly evident in son, a kind of music that emerged in the late nineteenth century, which mixes Spanish guitars with African drums. Son has a pulsing bass and lyrics that often deal with themes like love and patriotism. In the 1990s, son experienced a revival when a group of elderly musicians were featured on an album titled the *Buena Vista Social Club*.

Son is the basis for many musical styles, including rumba, mambo, and, later, salsa. Rumba shows strong African influences, while mambo incorporates big band swing music. In the 1950s, Beny Moré led a huge band that made mambo famous

An all-women group, Rumba Morena, plays at an outdoor concert in Havana's Cayo Hueso neighborhood.

The Buena Vista Social Club

Every few years, the world rediscovers Cuban music. The Buena Vista Social Club was long a gathering place for black residents of Havana who loved music and loved to dance. In the 1940s, the club attracted both local musicians and talent from around the world. The place was eventually shut down. By 1998, the Buena Vista had been closed for so long that no one was sure where it had been!

Ry Cooder, an American musician, traveled to Havana in 1996 to listen to some of the elderly Cuban musicians who had played at the club. Their music moved him. He persuaded them to make a recording, and the resulting album, named after the club, was an international hit.

Musicians who had played during the golden age of Cuban music, from 1930 to 1950, began once again to entertain. With Cooder's help, a number of musicians, including vocalist Ibrahim Ferrer, bassist Cachao López, and pianist Rubén González, became household names in Cuba and all over the world. A documentary film also called *Buena Vista Social Club* added to their fame.

The Cuban government approved of the music, mostly because it lured tourists to Cuba. Ironically, that same government had closed the social clubs after the revolution. Many musicians were forced to put away their instruments in order to make a living. Cooder found vocalist Ferrer working as a shoe shiner. The album and the movie spawned other work. The musicians toured the world, getting rave reviews wherever they performed.

Because of their advanced age, several of the musicians died within a few years of the recording. Meanwhile, the U.S. government fined Cooder, who played with the band as a guitarist, $25,000 for violating the U.S. trade embargo.

Celia Cruz won the 2003 Grammy Award for best salsa album. During her career, she won a total of seven Grammy and Latin Grammy awards.

in the United States. By the 1960s, Celia Cruz was known as the Queen of Salsa, a kind of music that mixes son, jazz, and other Latin forms for a sharper sound.

Many other musical styles also developed in Cuba. Guajira is earthy, forceful, rural acoustic music. *Música campesina*, improvised rural music, was a major influence on the popular son form. *Changuí* music, which is fast and percussive, also influenced the development of son.

Many of Cuba's greatest writers have dealt with themes of independence. Cuba's great patriot José Martí wrote dozens of books of poetry, plays, and essays. Alejo Carpentier (1904–1980), a poet, diplomat, and journalist, wrote from exile as an enemy of Fulgencio Batista. He mixed fact and fiction in books such as *The Kingdom of the World*. Poet Nicolás Guillén (1902–1989) drew on the culture of black Cubans. Miguel Barnet (1940–) has also focused on Cubans of African descent in *The Autobiography of a Runaway Slave* and other books.

Many writers from other countries made their home in Cuba before the revolution. American writer Ernest Hemingway lived in and loved Havana. He departed reluctantly with the coming of the revolution. While in Havana, he wrote *The Old Man and the Sea*, the tale of an elderly man who hooks a big fish and his feelings about life and death.

American novelist Ernest Hemingway speaks with the press at his home outside Havana in 1954. He had just been awarded the Nobel Prize for Literature.

Artistic Freedom?

When Fulgencio Batista was in charge of Cuba, the government did little to support artists. Batista believed that all artists were revolutionaries, so he did little to help them. After Fidel Castro took over, the Cuban government began offering strong support for arts and sports—but only in some fields. Dancers, athletes, and artists are encouraged and trained because they often suggest ideas but do not usually make overtly political statements. But not all artists receive the same support. Cuba once had several active film directors, but after the revolution, they were soon out of work. The government allows only films that promote its point of view.

Wilfredo Lam painted *Umbral* **in 1949–1950. It is in a museum in Paris, France.**

Art and Dance

Visual artists can draw on a rich palette in Cuba. Their paintings are filled with the rich greens of the nation's lush plant life and the many shades of blue of the Caribbean Sea and the Atlantic Ocean. Mix these colors with the artistic traditions of Spain and Africa, and conditions are ideal for vivid art.

Visitors to Cuba often return home with lovely paintings showing the artists' interpretations of city and rural areas. But not all Cuban art is landscape. Wilfredo Lam (1902–1982) drew on the Afro-Cuban tradition to paint black Cubans as he

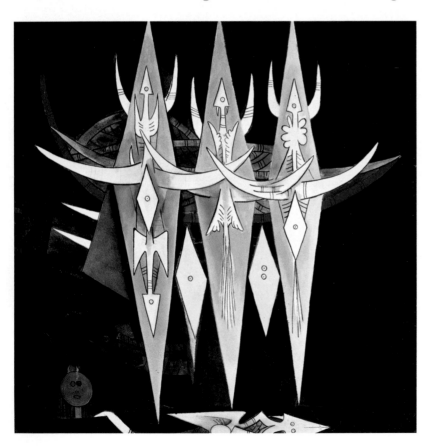

Alicia Alonso continued performing into her fifties. Here, she practices for a performance of *Giselle* in New York City in 1977.

felt they should look. His painting *The Jungle* (1943) hangs in New York City's Museum of Modern Art.

Cuba is home to a world-class ballet company. The National Ballet of Cuba was founded by Alicia Alonso (1920–), a ballerina who had studied in Havana and New York City. Alonso continued to choreograph well into her eighties despite poor vision. Alonso inspired several generations of young ballerinas all across the island. Modern dance is also thriving, in groups such as DanzAbierta and Danza Teatro Retazos.

The Museum of the Revolution

In downtown Havana stands a handsome stone building that was once the presidential palace. Just inside the entrance, visitors can see several bullet holes. These are souvenirs from an assassination attempt on Fulgencio Batista in 1957.

Items on display in the museum include bloody clothing worn by Fidel Castro's revolutionaries as well as their weapons. Exhibits also include berets worn by Ernesto "Che" Guevara, the Argentine doctor who joined Castro's revolutionary group in Mexico.

Granma, the leaky boat Castro and his fellow soldiers sailed from Mexico to Cuba to begin the revolution, is on display behind the palace. Also on exhibit are planes, tanks, and other vehicles used in the revolution and to stop the invasion at the Bay of Pigs in 1961.

Architecture

Like the bird-watchers who flock to Cuba each winter, tourists interested in architecture also flock to the island. Cuba has a rich history of architecture. Somewhere on the island, there are examples of virtually every school of architecture, including neoclassical, neo-Moorish, art deco, and baroque revival.

Neoclassical buildings imitate the stately buildings of ancient Greece and Rome, while neo-Moorish ones use

stained glass and fabrics with intricate, colorful designs. Art deco combines artistic values with a stripped-down, minimal look. Baroque revival architecture copies the fancy look and feel of European housing from 1550 to 1700.

A neoclassical building sits along the Plaza Mayor in the city of Sancti Spiritus.

Sports

Baseball has a long, rich history in Cuba. Nemisio Guillo, a Cuban who attended college in the United States, brought a ball and a bat back to Cuba in 1864. The first official game between Cuban teams took place in 1874, and a Cuban league was soon organized. The Spanish-American War, in 1898, gave Cubans and Americans many chances to play each other. Soon, Cuba was producing many great baseball players.

More than one hundred Cubans have played in the Major Leagues in the United States. For every Cuban big leaguer there are hundreds of Cuban children who love the game of baseball. Equipment may be old or nonexistent, but Cuban boys learn early how to hit, pitch, and run and steal bases.

Baseball is the national pastime of both Cuba and the United States. Professional baseball players are paid no more than US$20 a month in Cuba, but they can make millions in

Fans enjoy a baseball game at the Estadio Latinoamericano in Havana. The stadium holds about fifty-five thousand people.

El Duque

Many Cubans have played in the Major Leagues. The story of Orlando "El Duque" Hernández is typical. El Duque was a star pitcher in Cuba. He led his team to national championships and helped Cuba win a gold medal at the 1992 Summer Olympics.

Hernández fled Cuba aboard a rickety boat in 1997, landing in the Bahamas. The following year, he started playing with the New York Yankees. As of 2007, he had won ninety games playing for four different Major-League teams. Hernández lives in Miami, Florida, in the off-season.

the United States. Many Cuban baseball players have fled Cuba for the United States, where they have better opportunities.

Many Cubans also play basketball, volleyball, and soccer. Popular athletes in other sports include three-time Olympic gold medal winner Teófilo Stevenson (boxing), Félix Savon (boxing), and Ana Quirot (running).

Saying Good-bye to Cuba

Cuba restricts the right of most citizens to leave the country. Sometimes athletes, musicians, or government representatives who travel to other parts of the world defect, or refuse to go home. Instead, they ask a foreign government to allow them to stay. Many athletes have defected in order to earn more money. Fidel Castro called such actions "betrayal for money."

The Cuban government despises defections. Athletes representing Cuba in the 2007 Pan-American Games in Brazil left in a hurry beause their government feared mass defections. The Cubans left Brazil so quickly that the volleyball players did not even have time to collect their third-place medals. At the 1999 Pan-American Games in Canada, thirteen athletes defected.

A Taste of Life

Cubans dance during a concert in Havana.

O N WEEKEND EVENINGS, IN TOWNS SMALL AND LARGE, Cubans gather in plazas, the open areas in front of churches. They gather to dance and play dominoes, to see and be seen. Mostly, though, they just want to talk and laugh, because life in Cuba is open and social.

Opposite: **About 11 percent of Cubans are at least sixty-five years old.**

A girl poses in an elaborate dress during an event called a *quinceañera*. It is celebrated when a girl turns fifteen, marking the start of adulthood.

Dressing for Warm Weather

Cuba is a tropical island. It is warm year-round, so Cubans know how to dress for the heat. Children wear uniforms to school, but elsewhere they wear T-shirts and shorts. Women often wear bright clothes. When they go out, they favor fancy dresses, many of which are ruffled. Cuba is generally too warm for a coat and tie, so men wear a shirt known as a guayabera when they dress up. This is a white or pastel long-sleeve shirt with four pockets—two breast pockets and two pockets in front of the hips. Men don't tuck these shirts in, the better to stay cool. At parties and festivals, men often wear a white Cuban shirt and white pants. Younger people are fashion conscious. They try to buy the latest European or Asian styles, even if they have little money.

Rice and Beans and More

The most common meal in Cuba is rice and beans with fried plantains. A plantain is a starchy kind of banana that people cook like a root vegetable rather than eat like a fruit. A rice and beans dish usually includes garlic or other mild spices.

Pork is a mainstay in Cuba—Cubans say their pork is the best in the world. The most popular holiday main dish is a small, young pig roasted in sour orange juice or other fruit juices. Cubans also consume a lot of chicken, but beef is scarce and Cubans eat little seafood. Most fish caught in Cuba is exported. Popular drinks include locally grown coffee and fruit juice.

Fried plantains are popular throughout much of the Caribbean.

The Perfect Sandwich

Cubans have perfected the sandwich. Cuban sandwiches are made using a moist loaf of bread. Fillings include pork, ham, Swiss cheese, pickles, and yellow mustard. Once assembled, the sandwich is grilled in a press. Some people like tomato or lettuce on their sandwiches, but Cubans eat the vegetables separately.

East and West

Throughout Cuban history, ethnic groups settled in different parts of the country. Most Europeans lived in the cities. Enslaved Africans and poor Canary Islanders worked in rural areas. Today, this split is reflected in the foods of the regions.

A plate of tapas from a restaurant in Havana features olives, cheese, and sausage.

In western Cuban cooking, particularly in Havana, the food is like European fare. Cooks there make sauces such as *alcaparrado*, a sweet-sour sauce made with olives, raisins, and capers. Frequently cooked with ground meat, alcaparrado can be found on the table at most meals, much like ketchup in the United States or salsa in Mexico.

Another Spanish influence in the west is the serving of small dishes called *tapas*. Sometimes, tapas are appetizers; other times, Cubans eat a mix of tapas that serves

as the entire meal. Popular tapas ingredients include ham, chicken, beef, fish, and cheese.

In eastern Cuba, garlic, oregano, bay leaves, and onions flavor many dishes. Popular eastern dishes include beans and rice, fresh salads, meat with a variety of sauces, sausages, tamales, bean soup, corn stew, and plain rice. The most popular sauce is *mojo* or *mojito*, which is made with garlic, onion, spices, and bitter orange or lime juice.

East or west, dessert deserves special mention. Because sugarcane is such an important crop in Cuba, the most common dessert is *raspadura*, solidified sugarcane molasses. Other popular desserts include ground coconut boiled with sugar, anything made with guava paste, *churros* (fried-dough pastries), hot chocolate, marmalade, puddings, cakes, and, especially, custards such as flan. Ice cream is sold everywhere, often by street vendors.

Flan

Flan is a caramel dessert that has been around for hundreds of years. It may have originated in Spain or France and was brought to Cuba long ago by Europeans. Since it uses plenty of sugar, it's a natural for an island dessert.

Ingredients

1 ½ cups sugar

2 tablespoons hot water

4 eggs

2 cups heavy cream

1 cup milk

½ teaspoon vanilla

Directions

Preheat your oven to 350°F. In a saucepan, combine 1 cup of sugar and the hot water. Boil rapidly until the mixture is a deep amber color. Pour it into a 9-inch glass pie pan and coat the sides. Let cool. Meanwhile, beat the eggs in a large bowl. Add the remaining ½ cup sugar, heavy cream, milk, and vanilla, and mix thoroughly. Pour the mixture into the pie pan.

Place the pie pan in a large roasting pan. Carefully pour hot water into the roasting pan until it is halfway up the side of the pie pan. Bake for about 1 hour, until the flan is set. Refrigerate the flan for at least 4 hours. To serve it, flip it over and remove the pie pan, so the caramel syrup is on the top. Enjoy!

Housing

The kind of housing Cubans live in depends on where they live. In rural areas, many people live in *bohíos*. These are humble houses made of mud or clay with a roof covered in straw or reeds. They are poor shelter when bad weather strikes, but they are also easy to rebuild.

In small towns, most people live in houses made of concrete, limestone, or adobe (sun-dried mud bricks). In some places, people live in old mansions that sugarcane bosses built. These mansions have been split up so they can house several families. Many of them are in poor repair, and some have even partially collapsed.

After the revolution, there was a housing shortage. To solve this problem, many plain, concrete-slab apartment buildings were constructed. Some of the construction workers were unskilled volunteers, so these building were not always built well.

A row of concrete-slab houses lines a street in the city of Trinidad.

Education and health care are two areas in which Cuba receives great praise. In 1961, 250,000 schoolchildren were sent into the countryside to teach poor, rural people to read. This program was so successful that Cuba is among the world's most literate countries. In 1952, only 54 percent of Cubans were literate. Today, more than 99 percent of the population can read and write.

Cuba has one of the world's highest literacy rates. In 2005, 99.8 percent of the country's population over the age of fifteen could read.

A Cuban child starts school at age five and completes elementary school at age twelve. Secondary school (high school) then lasts to age seventeen. The national government provides all school supplies, school meals, and transportation. Cuban schools report an attendance rate of around 100 percent. All schoolchildren are required to wear uniforms.

Students return to class after attending a ceremony in Havana.

A doctor gives a lecture during a class at the Latin American School of Medical Sciences in Havana. The school trains students from countries throughout the Caribbean and the world.

Cuba has a total of forty-seven universities where students study technology, medicine, agriculture, history, chemistry, law, and other subjects. The University of Havana is Cuba's oldest and most prestigious university. It was founded in 1728.

Students at all levels of education spend time on public works projects. Those projects include building apartments, maintaining roads, and keeping their villages or cities clean.

Health Care

Cuban medicine emphasizes preventing disease before it strikes. This is the goal of doctors and nurses all over the world, but it is particularly important in Cuba because Cuba cannot manufacture all of the medicines it needs. Nor is Cuba able to afford many of the high-priced drugs available from Europe. Doctors work to keep people healthy, active, and aware of such common illnesses as sunstroke, dehydration, and childhood and tropical diseases. Cuba's preventive care works well: Cuban women live an average age of 79.5 years, and men live an average age of almost 75 years.

Many international organizations send medicine to Cuba for those in need. Some tourists also donate medicine and medical supplies while visiting the island.

Cuba has about three hundred hospitals, ranging from large urban sites filled with new equipment to simple clinics with a few beds in rural villages. The nation's sixty thousand doctors provide all treatment, which is free of charge. Cuban doctors also help people in other countries. During the 1980s, Cuba made friends abroad by quickly sending doctors to scenes of disasters and other emergencies.

Cuban doctors work in Haiti as part of an agreement between Haiti and Cuba. In 1998, some 130 Cuban medical personnel went to work in Haiti.

Cubans wave flags during a ceremony in Havana.

In Cuba, several national holidays commemorate pivotal moments during the revolution. They honor Castro's attack on the Moncada army barracks and the day after Batista fled the country. National holidays feature speeches, music, and crowds overflowing town squares. They present a great opportunity for Cubans to enjoy themselves. On national holidays, Cubans relax with neighbors, dance, snack, discuss local and national issues, and play dominoes.

Cuba has fifty-eight television stations. Every village of any size has a movie theater, and children and adults alike watch television and go to the movies. Baseball, soccer, basketball, boxing, and track and field are all popular spectator sports.

National Holidays

Liberation Day	January 1
Victory of the Armed Forces Day	January 2
Labor Day	May 1
National Revolution Day	July 25–27
Independence Day	October 10
Christmas	December 25

Crazy About Dominoes

The clatter of domino tiles is heard wherever Cubans gather to drink coffee, share a snack, or gossip. Probably conceived in China, dominoes were being used in Europe by the eighteenth century.

Dominoes can be made from ivory, bone, wood, plastic, or even cardboard. They are blank on one side and usually carry dots similar to dice on the other. The most common game involves players aligning matching dominoes, with a "bone pile" from which players draw pieces. The game has lots of variations, and there may be as few as 28 tiles or as many as 190 tiles in a set.

Some people in Cuba make their own dominoes, often drilling a hole in each piece. The holes allow them to run a wire through the pieces and carry them much the way that people carry keys. Amateur domino clubs with "domino nights" are common across the country.

Few Cubans can afford to travel abroad, and leaving the country on a vacation is something the government looks at with suspicion. No one is free to leave the country permanently, and those who make the attempt and fail may feel harsh discrimination by neighbors and local authorities.

Those who are successful in leaving count themselves lucky. They do what they can to help their relatives, sending money back to make the lives of those who remain in Cuba a little more pleasant. Someday, the U.S. embargo and travel ban may be lifted. Then, Cubans will be able to see their relatives more frequently, and Cubans and Americans will get to know one another again.

People crowd a city square in Cuba.

Timeline

Cuba History

Ciboney people settle in Cuba.	3500 B.C.–A.D. 1200
Taíno people arrive in Cuba.	ca. A.D. 900
Christopher Columbus lands in Cuba.	1492
Spaniard Diego Velásquez de Cuéllar invades Cuba.	1511
Spaniards bring the first enslaved Africans to Cuba.	1522
Black slaves in Haiti rebel, and some Haitian planters flee to Cuba.	1791
Cuban revolutionaries fight Spanish rule in the Ten Years' War.	1868–1878
Slavery is abolished in Cuba.	1886
José Martí leads a revolt against Spanish rule.	1895

World History

2500 B.C.	Egyptians build the pyramids and the Sphinx in Giza.
563 B.C.	The Buddha is born in India.
A.D. 313	The Roman emperor Constantine legalizes Christianity.
610	The Prophet Muhammad begins preaching a new religion called Islam.
1054	The Eastern (Orthodox) and Western (Roman Catholic) Churches break apart.
1095	The Crusades begin.
1215	King John seals the Magna Carta.
1300s	The Renaissance begins in Italy.
1347	The plague sweeps through Europe.
1453	Ottoman Turks capture Constantinople, conquering the Byzantine Empire.
1492	Columbus arrives in North America.
1500s	Reformers break away from the Catholic Church, and Protestantism is born.
1776	The U.S. Declaration of Independence is signed.
1789	The French Revolution begins.
1865	The American Civil War ends.
1879	The first practical light bulb is invented.

Cuba History

In the Spanish-American War, the United States supports Cuban revolutionaries and forces Spain to give up its claims to Cuba.	**1898**
The United States rules Cuba.	**1899–1902**
The Republic of Cuba is founded.	**1902**
The United States establishes a military base at Guantánamo.	**1903**
Fulgencio Batista seizes control of the government.	**1952**
Rebel forces under Fidel Castro begin a revolution against the Cuban government.	**1956**
Fulgencio Batista flees the country on December 31.	**1958**
Fidel Castro takes control of the government.	**1959**
The U.S. places an economic embargo on Cuba to pressure it into changing its communist system.	**1960**
American-trained Cubans invade at the Bay of Pigs; Castro's forces quickly defeat them.	**1961**
The United States forces the Soviet Union to remove missiles from Cuba.	**1962**
Cuba adopts a new constitution that establishes the Communist Party as the only political party.	**1976**
Cuba's economy begins to suffer as the Soviet Union collapses.	**1991**
The government allows some Cubans to start privately owned businesses.	**1993**
Pope John Paul II visits Cuba, resulting in more religious freedom.	**1998**
Illness forces Fidel Castro to hand over power to his brother, Raúl.	**2006**
Fidel Castro officially resigns as president.	**2008**

World History

1914	World War I begins.
1917	The Bolshevik Revolution brings communism to Russia.
1929	A worldwide economic depression begins.
1939	World War II begins.
1945	World War II ends.
1957	The Vietnam War begins.
1969	Humans land on the Moon.
1975	The Vietnam War ends.
1989	The Berlin Wall is torn down as communism crumbles in Eastern Europe.
1991	The Soviet Union breaks into separate countries.
2001	Terrorists attack the World Trade Center in New York City and the Pentagon in Arlington, Virginia.

Fast Facts

Official name: República de Cuba (Republic of Cuba)

Capital: Havana

Official language: Spanish

Havana

Cuba's flag

Valle de Viñales

Official religion:	None
Year of founding:	1902
National anthem:	"La Bayamesa" ("The Bayamo Song")
Government:	Communist state with a one-house legislature
Chief of state:	President
Head of government:	President
Area:	42,804 square miles (110,861 sq km)
Greatest distance east to west:	708 miles (1,139 km)
Greatest distance north to south:	135 miles (217 km)
Bordering countries:	None
Highest elevation:	Pico Turquino, 6,542 feet (1,994 m)
Lowest elevation:	Sea level, along the coast
Average high temperatures:	In Havana, 89°F (32°C) in August; 75°F (24°C) in January
Average annual rainfall:	More than 70 inches (180 cm) in the mountains, 40 inches (100 cm) in the lowlands
National population (2007 est.):	11,394,043

Museum of the Revolution

Currency

Population of largest cities:

Havana	2,686,000
Santiago de Cuba	554,400
Camagüey	354,400
Holguín	319,300
Guantánamo	274,300

Famous landmarks:

▶ *Cueva de Punta del Este*, Isla de la Juventud

▶ *El Morro*, Havana

▶ *Museum of the Revolution*, Havana

▶ *Valle de Viñales*, Pinar del Río

▶ *Zapata Swamp*, Zapata Peninsula

Industry: Service industries, such as banking, education, and healthcare, make up the largest part of Cuba's economy. Tourism is Cuba's fastest-growing service industry, with foreign tourists spending more than US$2 billion annually in Cuba. Sugar is Cuba's leading manufactured product. Cigars, oil, food products, medicines, cement products, and textiles are other leading manufactured goods. Cuba's leading mined products are nickel and chromite. Important agricultural products include sugarcane, rice, tobacco, and citrus fruits.

Currency: There are two types of currency in Cuba: the peso and the convertible peso. In 2008, US$1 equaled 23 pesos, and 1 peso equaled 4 cents. One convertible peso equaled about 24 pesos and US$1.08.

Weights and measures: The metric system is widely used.

Literacy rate: 99%

Cubans

Celia Cruz

Common Spanish words and phrases:

buenos días	hello/good day
buenas noches	good evening/night
adiós	good-bye
sí	yes
no	no
por favor	please
gracias	thank you
¿cuánto?	how much?
¿cuántos?	how many?
¿Dónde está . . . ?	Where is . . . ?
¿Qué hora es?	What time is it?

Famous Cubans:

Alicia Alonso (1920–)
Ballerina and choreographer

Fulgencio Batista (1901–1973)
Dictator

Fidel Castro (1926–)
Revolutionary and president

Celia Cruz (1924–2003)
Singer

Ibrahim Ferrer (1927–2005)
Musician

Nicolás Guillén (1902–1989)
Poet

Orlando Hernández (1965–)
Baseball player

Wilfredo Lam (1902–1982)
Painter

José Martí (1853–1895)
Political leader and writer

To Find Out More

Books

▶ Ada, Alma Flor. *Under the Royal Palms*. New York: Atheneum, 1998.

▶ Campbell, Fiona Kumari. *Cuba in Pictures*. Minneapolis: Lerner, 2005.

▶ Gay, Kathlyn. *Leaving Cuba: Operation Pedro*. Brookfield, CT: Twenty-First Century Books, 2000.

▶ Markel, Rita J. *Fidel Castro's Cuba*. Minneapolis: Lerner, 2007.

▶ Schreier, Alta. *A Visit to Cuba*. Chicago: Heinemann Library, 2001.

Audio

▶ *Buena Vista Social Club*. Nonesuch, 1997.

▶ Cruz, Celia. *100% Azucar! The Best of Celia Cruz con la Sonora Matancera*. Rhino/Wea, 1997.

▶ Moré, Benny. *Lo Mejor de lo Mejor*. Sony International, 2001.

Web Sites

▶ **Cuba.com**
www.Cuba.com
*For information about the geography,
travel, U.S. restrictions, weather,
shopping, and tourism.*

▶ **CubaWeb Directory About Cuba**
www.cubaweb.cu/
*A good reference on tourism, culture,
and national news.*

▶ **The World Factbook: Cuba**
www.cia.gov/library/publications/
the-world-factbook/geos/cu.html
*To find lots of basic information and
statistics on Cuba.*

Organizations and Embassies

▶ **Embassy of Cuba in Canada**
388 Main Street
Ottawa, Ontario K1S 1E3
Canada
613/563-0141
http://embacu.cubaminrex.cu/
Default.aspx?tabid=73

Index

Page numbers in *italics* indicate illustrations.

Guillén, Nicolás, 105, 133
Guillo, Nemisio, 109
Gulf of Guacanayabo, 23
Gulf of Mexico, *19*

H

Haiti, 18, 39, 46, 82–83, *124*
Hatuey (Taíno leader), 43, *43*
Havana, 9, 18, 19, *19*, 26, 27, 34, 44,
   44, 45, 54, 62, 65, 68–69, *68*, *69*,
   74, *79*, *83*, *87*, *88*, *90*, *94*, *97*,
   98, *100*, *101*, *102*, 103, *105*,
   108, *110*, *113*, *117*, *121*, *122*,
   125. See also cities.
health care, 58, 76, 77, 79, 88, *88*,
   123–124, *123*, *124*
Hemingway, Ernest, 105, *105*
Hernández, Orlando "El Duque,"
   111, *111*, 133
Hershey Company, *54*
Hispaniola, 18
historical maps. *See also* maps.
   European exploration, *42*
   Spanish-American War, *49*
Holguín, 27, 87
Hotel Nacional de Cuba, *74*
housing, 14, 118–119
hurricanes, 25, 62
hutia (rodent), 31, *31*

I

insect life, 31, 35
Isabel Rubio, *24*
Isla de la Juventud, 18, 20, *33*, 36, 39

J

Jamaica, 83
John Paul II (pope), 93, *93*
Judaism, 98, *98*
judicial branch of government,
   64, 65–66, *65*

K

Kennedy, John F., 56
King's Gardens (islands), 22
Kwong Wah Po newspaper, *83*

L

"La Bayamesa" ("The Bayamo
   Song"), 67
Lam, Wilfredo, 106–107, *106*, 133
languages, 89
Lanier Swamp, *33*
Latin American School of Medical
   Sciences, *122*
Lau, Israel Meir, *98*
legislative branch of government, 64
leopard dwarf boa, *28*
Lesser Antilles, 18
limestone, 20, *20*
literature, 105, *105*
Little Havana (Miami, Florida), 86
López, Cachao, 103

M

Maceo y Grajales, Antonio, 48
Machado, Gerardo, 50, *50*
Madruga, 96
Malecón seawall, 69, *101*
mambo music, 102
manatees, 32, *32*
mangrove forests, 37, *37*
Mantanzas, *75*
manufacturing, 26, 75–76
maps. *See also* historical maps.
   geopolitical, *13*
   Havana, *69*
   population density, *87*
   resources, *77*
   topographical, *18*
marine life, 29, *29*, 30, *30*, 32, *32*,
   37, 40, 76, *76*
mariposa lily (national flower), 37, *37*

Martí, José, 9–11, *10*, 48, 105, 133
Matanzas Province, 21
Matos, Huber, 66
medicines, 76
metric system, 78
military, 22, *22*, 51, 56, 67, *67*, 86
mining, 43, 58, 76, 77, 79, 83
Ministry of Foreign Affairs, 64
Ministry of Justice, 64
Moa, *26*, 58
mojo sauce, 117
Moncada army barracks, 52, 63, 125
Moré, Beny, 102
movie theaters, 125
music, 14, 15, 41, 101–102, *101*,
   102, 103, *103*, 104, *104*, 125
música campesina (improvised
   music), 104
Muslims, 98

N

national anthem, 67
National Assembly of People's Power,
   62, *62*, 63, 64–65
National Ballet of Cuba, *100*, 107
national bird, 35, *35*
national capitol, *60*
national constitution, 61, 63, 64
national flag, 61, *61*
national flower, 37, *37*
national holidays, 125, *125*
national parks, 21
national tree, 36, *36*
naval blockade, 56
neoclassical architecture, 108, *109*
neo-Moorish architecture, 108–109

O

Ocampo, Sebastián de, *42*
oil, 79, *79*
Olympic Games, 111

Meet the Author

DAVID K. WRIGHT has written dozens of nonfiction books for both young people and adults, including *Albania*, *Brunei*, *Burma*, and *Vietnam* in Scholastic's Enchantment of the World series. He has also written books on subjects ranging from motorcycles to world travels to the Vietnam War.

"Writing *Cuba* was a real eye-opener for me," he says. "A lot of the things of everyday American life—music, food, politics—have been influenced by Cuba and Cubans. I also learned more about how the United States has played an important part in Cuban affairs for several centuries."

Wright speaks basic Spanish and interviewed several people who travel frequently to Cuba.

Wright lives in Madison, Wisconsin. He is married and has two grown children, two dogs, and two cats.

Photo Credits

Alamy Images: 36 (Arco Images), 116 (John Birdsall), 37 bottom (Content Mine International), 37 top (Chris Dennis), 86 (Jeff Greenberg), 20, 131 bottom (Robert Harding Picture Library), 7 bottom, 81 (Hemis), 84 (Tommy Huynh), 27 top (Melvyn Longhurst), 39 (Melba Photo Agency), 115 (MShields Photos), 117 (Swerve), 26 (Mireille Vautier), 27 bottom (Rawdon Wyatt)

AP Images: 65 (Jose Goitia), 93 (Paul Hanna/Pool), 100 (Cristobal Herrera), 124 (Daniel Morel), 103 (Stuart Ramson), 59 (Lynne Sladky), 105, 107

Art Resource, NY: 43 (Bildarchiv Preussuscher Kulturbesitz), 40 (The Metropolitan Museum of Art)

Bridgeman Art Library International Ltd., London/New York: 106 (Wilfredo Lam/ Musee National d'Art Moderne, Centre Pompidou, Paris, France/Peter Willi)

Corbis Images: 10, 50, 51, 55, 82 (Bettmann), 108, 132 top (Michael Brennan), 99 (Claudia Daut/Reuters), 73, 132 bottom (George B. Diebold), 57, 101 (Alejandro Ernesto/epa), 9, 38 (Owen Franken), 80 (Patrick Frilet/Hemis), 127, 133 top (Philippe Giraud), 17 (Frans Lemmens/zefa), 30 (Amos Nachoum), 2 (Jose Fuste Raga), 104, 133 bottom (Reuters), 19 (Al Rod), 125 (Heriberto Rodriguez/Reuters), 126 (Gregor Schuster/zefa), 102, 113 (Peter Turnley), 88 (Peter Turnley for Harper's), 46

Danita Delimont Stock Photography/ Jon Arnold: back cover, cover, 6

Getty Images: 98 (AFP), 89 (Rodrigo Arangua), 23, 75 (Jose Azel/Aurora), 118 (Thomas Barwick), 12 (Angelo Cavalli), 76 (Francoise De Mulder/Roger Viollet), 85 (Gregory Ewald/U.S. Coast Guard), 74 (Stephen Ferry/Liason), 120 (Bruno Morandi), 25 (NOAA), 122 (Joe Raedle), 79 (Jorge Rey), 63, 94, 123 (Adalberto Roque/AFP), 92 (STR/ AFP), 66 (Robert Sullivan/AFP), 54 (Three Lions), 71, 110 (Travel Ink), 21 (Steve Winter)

Inmagine: 61, 131 top

Lonely Planet Images: 119 (Tim Hughes), 112 (Shannon Bruce Nace)

Magnum Photos: 95, 114 (Abbas), 53 (Rene Burri), 58, 72 (David Alan Harvey), 70, 96 (Thomas Hoepker)

Minden Pictures: 29 (Jurgen Freund/npl), 32 bottom (Todd Pusser/npl)

Nature Picture Library Ltd.: 11 (Willem Kolvoort), 7 top, 16 (David Noton), 8 (Mike Potts)

NEWSCOM/Vanessa Bauza: 97

Photoshot: 32 top, 34 (James Carmichael Jr.), 31, 33, 35 bottom, 35 top (Lee Dalton), 41 (Mel Longhurst), 28 (Chris Mattison)

Reuters: 15, 24, 62, 121 (Claudia Daut), 67 (Enrique de la Osa), 22, 78, 83, 91, 111

Robert Harding World Imagery/Neil Emmerson: 68, 130 left

The Art Archive/Picture Desk: 48 (Culver Pictures), 49 top (Gianni Dagli Orti), 47 (Gianni Dagli Orti/Biblioteca Nacional Madrid), 44, 90 (Nicolas Sapieha), 60 (Neil Setchfeld), 109 (Mireille Vautier), 45

The Granger Collection, New York: 14, 42 bottom, 52.

Maps by XNR Productions, Inc.